# STILL STRAPPED

By

Sharon D. Smith

# Still Strapped

by

Sharon D. Smith

Copyright © 2011 by Sharon D. Smith

ISBN 978-1-257-78935-1

Manufactured in the United States of America

Edited by Sharon D. Smith, M.A. & Kristal M. Davis, M.Ed.
Cover Photography by
Annamadit Photography and Graphic Designs
Atlanta, Ga.

# STILL STRAPPED

# Book Review

"The Strapped series can be viewed as a literary laboratory, where dominant lesbians can secretly and unapologetically experience the laughter, love, and sexual intensity of two stud women, Silk and Taz. Sharon D. Smith continues to deliver a sneak peek behind closed doors to openly view the perils and joys of a stud loving another stud. The second book, Still Strapped, picks up where the first installment of the Strapped series leaves off. This time, the S4S relationship is viewed through the eyes of Silk, who is more edgy, street smart, and dominant than Taz....

Smith has written a ground breaking book series for the lesbian community, especially African American lesbians. She carefully and artistically creates an intermarriage between social issues that plague the LGBTQ community as a whole with issues that are specific to African American lesbians in the life. The Strapped series will undoubtedly become the cornerstone for discussing lesbian issues within literary coursework that focuses on women's studies in college classrooms.    -- Kristal M. Davis, M.Ed.

# Outside the Box

"My friends kept telling me studs don't date studs. You gotta date a femme. I could not find it in the rulebook, so I kept on loving who[m]ever loved me....It has always struck me strange that Black folks who have traditionally been the most segregated against and prejudiced and judged against, continue to be the strongest and most condemnatory in their own communities." --A.S., Washington, D.C.

"I finally admitted to myself I prefer butches more than aggressive femmes...I just never pursued another butch until now because of the community's negative responses [and] I was never made aware [that] others like myself existed." --A.B., Maryland

"If a femme wants to be with a femme, [they're] ready to put it on HBO...But if [two] studs [are] together, they turn their noses like it's the end of the world...I'm getting tired of this shit. Why don't everybody just drop the labels and grow up!" --R.H., Somewhere in the U.S.

## An Interview with Kai "The Stud Slayer" Brown
February 2011

SS: Were you pressured by your peers to "stay in your lane" and did you ever think they may have been right? How did you truly know that you wanted to be with a stud and no one else?

KB: I've never been the type to let anyone influence what I do. People were definitely shocked when I told them, but they also knew that I did what I wanted. I knew I only wanted to date studs exclusively when I connected with one and I liked the easy-going way we had with each other. I grew to really appreciate another stud's swag, especially if it was similar to mine. The connection had me hooked.

SS: What were some of the challenges you faced in any of your long-term S4S relationships?

KB: The biggest challenge for me was finding the type of stud I wanted. There were certain qualities I was looking for and I wasn't willing to settle. So I dated [and] fucked studs for a long time, but now I'm in my first true relationship with my current boifriend. But in general, I think a lot of S4S studs try to find a balance between the two strong personalities. Studs tend to want to be in control and you have to be willing to compromise and concede on some issues. That may be a real challenge for some. And of course social acceptance is a major challenge.

SS: How would you describe the opinions that others within our community have of you and your personal preferences?

KB: Well, my first thought is a) Why do you care? and b) It's none of your business. But the Black lesbian community's opinions of S4S in general are born out of insecurities and unfamiliarity. Black people are slow to change and quick to judge. Some femmes see S4S as a challenge to their desirability to other studs. Non S4S studs see it as a threat to their masculine identity because when approached by one, they get real defensive and some even violent.

SS: Why do you feel most people are not open to S4S relationships?

KB: Simply put, S4S isn't the norm for our community. It's not common and rarely seen. It breaks the long-standing dynamic of stud/femme relationships. I think mainstream Black lesbians feel that stud-4-stud casts a negative [and] more ultra-masculine light on the community. They associate S4S with the old school term "bull-daggers." Black lesbians think straight people understand stud/femme relationships more because it looks a lot like them, hence making them more acceptable.

SS: Where are S4S relationships most visible? Do you think that equates to "acceptance" or "tolerance?"

KB: S4S relationships are most visible within the White lesbian community. White butch lesbians are the most common image of lesbianism to the general public. I think it's not only accepted, but tolerated as well. Even Black people accept that visual for White lesbians, but not for us! We rebuke that image so much, that we did the exact opposite and embraced more heterosexual-like roles such as stud/femme so as to be more accepted by our families and community.

SS: Would you feel comfortable going with your partner to a gay pride parade or event in Atlanta or some other Southern city? What about a Northern city?

KB: I'm a Southern boi and I'm familiar with the attitudes of the Southern states. Change is very slow down there, but I would totally be comfortable being out and proud in Atlanta as well as New York or another northern state. People are always gonna be curious and/or standoffish about what they don't know. If I can inspire someone else to show their truth, then any negativity I may encounter will be worth it.

8

SS: How do people look at you when you're out in public with your partner? How does it make you feel? Do they ever say anything to you? If so, what kind of things do they say?

KB: People definitely stared in the beginning when we first got together. Femmes gave us the most grief. They've said some of the most awful things. We've been called "fags," "bitches," "punks," and "weird." One femme asked "How could you possibly not like femmes? What's wrong with you?" Or my favorite, "What a fuckin' waste!" I was more shocked than angry, but I learned to chalk it up to jealousy. [It's] kinda like how a straight woman feels when she sees two fine ass gay men that are together. White lesbians embrace us because they rarely see Black S4S. I'm a big boi, so "str8" studs don't say much within earshot of me. Now gay men, they love us. I feel most comfortable around them because they understand. It's been 3 years now and we're known in DC so it's no thing when we step out.

SS: What is the one thing you would really like people to know about S4S relationships?

KB: People, especially femmes, seem to think that just because a stud likes to be penetrated by another stud that she's weak, soft, or less of a stud. We are definitely comfortable in our masculinity or we wouldn't be dating another stud to begin with. But while we are on this, I would also like for people to know that we are not out to "turn" any studs out so it annoys me when non S4S studs get their boxers in a bunch when they are around or are approached by an S4S stud. We normally know who's down and who's not so the likelihood of us running up on you improper is slim to none. And, if we do, all you have to say is "not my thing" and we will back off. Anything more than that and you're showing your insecurities.

SS: What are some of the main differences between an S4S relationship and an S4F relationship?

KB: Our relationship has many dimensions. She's not only my lover, but my BEST friend, road dog, wing man, therapist, whatever I need her to be. There are times we are out together and you would never know we were together because we're flirting with other women or doing our thing. I've NEVER had that kind of freedom with a femme where I could approach another woman and have a conversation without there being drama. I think there are a lot less insecurities in S4S relationships because the mentalities are so much alike. S4S couples can relate to the everyday struggles of just being a stud, like being mistaken for a man in public bathrooms or being turned down for a job because you decided to be you and not wear a dress for the money. It's been my experience that studs don't require as much attention and maintenance as femmes.

For me, the biggest difference has been the sex. I think it's more raw and honest because we are not bound by the "rules" that studs can't and shouldn't experience pleasure or submit in any way.

SS: Do you feel there is real unity in the LGBT community? What steps do you think need to be taken to achieve acceptance of S4S relationships? Do you feel like you really fit within the lesbian community given your personal preferences?

KB: No, I don't think there is unity within the LGBT community. There's blatant racism and sexism. Lesbians, gays, Blacks, and Whites rarely party or hang out as one. The gay community is separated by the haves and have-nots as well. As with any subculture, we are a direct representation of mainstream society. The only way S4S in the Black community will be accepted and respected is if we continue to come out and be proud about who we love. We need to open our minds and get out of these archaic boxes about sexuality and identity. The world is clearly not Black and White, neither is sexuality. Not only do I feel like I don't fit in this community because of my preferences, but I represent a large subset that has yet to bust on the scene. At the end of the day we are still two women no matter how we identify.

SS: What was your first intimate encounter like? Was it what you expected? How did it compare to any other type of relationship you've had in your adult life?

KB: WOW, that was oh so long ago! LOL. We played basketball together. There was definitely some sexual tension in the air and we knew it. I let her know I wanted her by letting my hand linger on her ass when I smacked it during the game. Or, I would grab her thigh while posting up in the paint. She never gave me a sign that she didn't like it so I didn't stop. I was at her house one day and we were chillin' on the couch. She brushed her leg against mine and I looked at her. Next thing you know, the Jordans and the shorts were on the floor and it was on! It was everything I knew it would be. It was hot, raw, sexy, greedy, [and] needy. She wasn't out about letting another stud fuck her so we saw each other on the sly until I joined the Marine Corps. Sadly we lost touch. I think about her every now and then. It was the first time I felt totally sexually free without the confines of bullshit rules and it felt great.

SS: Each culture and subculture in America has its own beliefs, customs, and traditions. Are there any unique traditions, terms, values, or ideologies in S4S culture?

KB: There's nothin' extra special about S4S. Aside from wearing the same type of clothes and swag, we are no different from any other gay couple. Most S4S are not exclusively stud4stud. In fact, the majority date femmes as well. A lot of us identify with gay men, so we use a lot of their terms such as top and bottom (aggressive/submissive) & trade (jump off). We call each other "bois," playing off the male identifier of boy. Ironically, a lot of S4S also pattern their relationships from stud and femme ones. It's rare to see two top bois together, but you will almost always recognize the top and bottom couple or even two bottom bois together. I like breaking all the rules and being totally different so I prefer top bois like myself and I don't date femmes at all.

SS: What role does race play in S4S relationships? Do you think Whites are more successful/loving in their S4S relationships than African Americans?

KB: Race plays a HUGE role in S4S relationships. Black people are bogged down with appearances and what their peers think, whereas White people not only encourage, but cherish being different. Things that may not be widely accepted in our community are shunned and hidden. The Black gay community is heavily steeped in male/female and stud/femme roles as patterned after our straight brothas and sistahs. So, if two Black studs do make it to the point that they want to be together openly, the odds of them staying [together]…are slim because of the cultural pressures to conform. White butch on butch lesbians are the most common image of lesbianism so White S4S couples have a higher success rate because they have a reference and they're less likely to encounter as much hostility from their peers, community, [and] family.

SS: What advice would you give to studs struggling with the decision to live in their truth and be with the person they really want to be with? How can studs who are not interested in S4S relationships still support those who want to be?

KB: Only YOU can live your life. If you're worrying about what everyone else says or thinks about you, then you're not living a full life. I was out as gay in the Marine Corps long before DADT (Don't Ask, Don't Tell) was even thought about being repealed. You know what I found? Who I slept with didn't matter. I was liked and respected because of who I was, not who I slept with. That positive reaction was the springboard to be vocal about S4S. It takes a lot of courage to be who you are instead of what other people want you to be. When those people leave, you will be alone with you. Can you live with that person? Non S4S can support us by just accepting and RESPECTING our choices. If you can't do that, just mind ya business.

*To learn more about The Stud Slayer and her upcoming events or to schedule a guest appearance, visit her at Facebook/studslayer.*

My advice for any self-identifying stud who is physically, emotionally, and sexually attracted to another self-identifying stud is to do what makes you happy. One of the greatest mistakes you can make in life is sacrificing your own happiness and well-being to please those who are not feeding you, funding you, or....you get the idea. I encourage all lesbians, particularly S4S lesbians, to live in truth, whatever that may mean to you.

-- Sharon D. Smith

# Serenity

*There were moments I wished I was dead because living seemed like
a desperate attempt to hold on to a world that didn't belong to me.
Those were the moments I felt alone and empty. It was a careful mix
of faith, fortune, and fighting that got me through it all.*

## Chapter 1

I woke up to my usual 5:45AM hot hazelnut and caramel coffee, this time with double whipped cream and a single mint leaf for extra flavor. Coffee was a must for me before my morning run. It put me in just the right mood to do what I needed to do and stay focused. A morning without it and the smooth, sweet stench of a vanilla Black and Mild meant trouble for everyone around me.

I put on my black and red bandana I wore every

time I had a big boxing match, a red Reebok t-shirt, black jogging pants, and a pair of black Reebok cross-trainers. I checked in on Alex and Taylor to make sure they were still sleeping, kissed them on the forehead like I do every morning I wake up, and set out for a relaxing five mile run.

The cool, morning air was refreshing. As the moon gave way to a cloudless sky and burnt orange sunrise, I thought about my day. I hoped for a day of drama-free fun and hanging out with Taz watching the NFL playoffs. I was excited about meeting Preacher for the first time, too. I wasn't sure how we'd get along, but I was optimistic. Taz said Preacher was a "tell-it-like-it-is" type of person, one who wouldn't bite her tongue just because you were her friend. I could respect that because I was the same way. I didn't see the point in holding back, especially if somebody deserved to be checked.

I ran about three miles before stopping at the muddy banks of Cooper Lake. The sunlight's reflection across the still water captured my attention. I stood motionless with my hands clasped behind my head and watched the sun make its final ascent. I watched as a tiny white bird trouble the water as it skipped across the lake's surface then resumed its morning flight. I couldn't help but stare at the bird as it disappeared over the trees. Its wings were fully outstretched while it carelessly glided across the morning sky. For a split second, I was jealous. I longed for the same feeling of freedom and innocence as that little bird with its mind on nothing but the wind as it effortlessly carried him to his next destination. I longed for the day I, too, could live my life as free as that bird and not be so tied down to the things around me. I was tired and stressed out.

I felt like a kid again as I sat Indian style on the cool, wet grass next to a tall oak tree. I was so lost in my own thoughts, I didn't care about the fresh morning dew dampening my pants or the squirrels scurrying past me in search of food and fun. As I sat there, so many scenes of my life flashed before me. There were moments of happiness and moments of regrets. There were moments of shame and disappointment. There were moments I wished I was dead because living seemed like a desperate attempt to hold on to a world that didn't belong to me. Those were the moments I felt alone and empty. It was a careful mix of faith, fortune, and fighting that got me through it all.

I sat there for what seemed like hours just thinking back over my life. My sister's death, my strange relationship with Taz, the custody battle for Alex and Taylor, and living a fucked up double life seemed too much for me to handle. But like most people I knew, I was making it work for me the best way I knew how. I was getting by, but that wasn't enough. As I continued to think about my journey and how I wished things were different, the sound of passing cars and trucks was a sudden, harsh reminder that it was time for me to go home and get back to reality.

By the time I showered and changed into an Atlanta Dream jogging suit and hat, it was 9 o'clock. Taz and I helped the girls get ready so they could spend an hour with Malcolm before heading to their friend's house for the day.

It would have been Malcolm's first time seeing the girls unsupervised. He calmed down a lot since the trial. He seemed more open and relaxed. He was almost normal. We weren't best friends, but we managed to be cordial. For us, that was progress. We dropped the girls off at the IHOP on Main Street to meet Malcolm and said we'd return in an hour to pick them up and take them to their friend's house.

When we returned, Taz and I played a few rounds of 8-ball just to pass the time away. I looked at my watch. It was 12:30. I nervously reached for a new pack of vanilla Black and Mild's I had hidden in my jacket pocket. Taz always said I was killing myself with these cancer sticks, but smoking was how I dealt with the tough things in my

21

life. It was therapeutic. At the end of a long day, a cold beer and a good smoke was the perfect fix. I never went as far as smoking the heavy stuff because it wasn't my thing. However, I needed something to quickly calm my nerves right now.

I watched as Taz lined up for her third attempt at the 8-ball. This time, she called a three-cushion shot to the corner pocket. It was an impossible shot to make, but she rarely backed down from a challenge. She was tough, despite her outward calm, white-boy persona and short stature.

"Sometime today, Counselor," I teased as she chalked up. "Ol' girl will be here soon."

"Look," she said. "This takes time. You never rush the perfect shot. Haven't I taught you anything?"

"Whatever," I sighed and took another quick puff then blew a stream of gray smoke rings into the air above the pool table.

I looked as she leaned across the table. She had

one foot on the floor and the other raised just enough to get a little leverage. She wore my Ole Miss baseball cap turned to the back and matching sweatshirt, along with a pair of Abercrombie jeans I bought her a few weeks ago after signing her newest client, Nina Alvarez, a hot-shot basketball player from Miami. She glanced just over the top of her black, thin-rimmed Oakley glasses, which she didn't wear often, claiming they made her look like a nerd. I often told her nerds were the next best thing to some good head and a good smoke, at least in my world they were. I loved them all. She aimed and hit the cue ball against the 8-ball. The 8-ball had lost momentum after hitting the third rail, but had just enough spin left to fall in its rightful pocket.

"Yes! Another win!" Taz yelled in excitement as she turned the cap around to the front. "You're losing your touch, babe. What's up with you? I'm up three games."

"Congratulations," I said sarcastically. "You're the

23

man!" I looked at my watch again. It was 12:45.

"Be cool," Taz encouraged me. "Preacher's not that bad. She's cool and I'm sure she'll like you. You're making me nervous."

Taz had a way of making things seem better than what they really were. She'd smile, look at me with her dark brown bedroom eyes, say something crazy, and then the whole world was right again. I never really experienced that before. I was so used to people telling me to "man up." Sometimes that style of comfort worked. Sometimes it didn't. Most times, it left me feeling even more disappointed and confused about the way I wanted to live my life. I was always the emotional type, but I learned how to contain even the deepest hurts and regrets. I refused to cry and I refused to let anybody think I was soft.

Regardless of what others said, Taz was my nigga! She was down for me from the beginning. I'm sure it wasn't the easiest task in the world. Even after all the

24

bullshit I put her through with that trifling ass Zodiac and her failed three-year relationship with her "Reece Cup," Taz was faithful to me, and the girls. She was a good friend, one I could really trust.

Taz knew about my past, but there were still pages of my life I wasn't ready to share with her. It wasn't because I was afraid, at least not totally. I didn't think she was ready to hear the whole truth and learn about the real me behind the basketball jerseys and tailored Armani suits she liked so much. I didn't think she was ready for what she really needed to know about me. It was hard enough for me to tell Taz about Zodiac. She took it better than I thought, but I couldn't imagine how she would react if she knew about some of my past relationships or the things Reece shared with me when she wasn't around. I wanted to tell her everything, but I couldn't. It never seemed to be the right time.

Sometimes I wondered how Taz and I even got to this point. We started out as two shit-talkers on the basketball court and moved into our own world, one in which the new Taz was unearthed and I was hopelessly buried in a lie – again! It was a lie I wasn't sure I could go through a second time around. After Dominic, I said "never the fuck again!" I refused to put myself through the drama of another relationship with studs who have more issues than these silly femmes I chose not to deal with. Despite my apprehensions, I went in hard. I thought Taz was worth the sacrifices I knew I'd have to make. She was worth the struggle and the memories that came to the forefront of my mind every day. I loved her and there was no question about that. I figured she felt the same way about me.

"How much does Preacher know about me?" I asked Taz as we set up for another game. "What have you told her?"

"Everything is cool," Taz responded in her usual, evasive way.

"That's not answering my question. What have

you told her?"

I needed to know how up front Taz was with Preacher. After all, they were best friends. They shared everything, much like myself and the two people I call true friends, Mike and Chris. I knew Taz hadn't told anyone else about us except Preacher, which made things more complicated.

Whenever Taz and I went out or hung with her crew, I was always the "workout partner," a cousin from some ten square mile town in Georgia that nobody heard of, or the next big athlete she was working with to seal the deal on a million-dollar contract. I knew this was new territory for Taz and I didn't want to shake her world more than I already had. I wanted her to be comfortable so I played the part, said my rehearsed lines, and made a quick, quiet exit. I grew accustomed to the act for the sake of our relationship, and our friendship. But my role as just somebody Taz knew or distant family member was quickly becoming a nuisance. I wanted more. I needed more and I felt that at this point, I deserved more.

"Relax," Taz instructed.

"One day you'll answer my questions directly," I commented. "A simple question deserves at least a simple answer."

Just as Taz was about to hug me and give me some more locker room pep talk about calming down, the doorbell rang. My heart fell from my chest. I felt a surge of adrenaline rush violently through my body. Normally I was cool when it came to meeting new people, but this time was different. I hung my cue stick on the rack and ran upstairs without delay.

When I opened the door, Preacher greeted me with a firm handshake. She took off her dark sunglasses and smiled slyly. She wasn't unattractive, but she had a little thugness about her that wasn't quite my speed. Had I known her a few years ago, she may have been just the right one to get my full attention and maybe even a little one-on-one play.

She had on a black and red throwback Atlanta Falcons cap that barely covered her thick, shoulder-length braids. She wore a matching Michael Vick jersey and a pair of baggy, black Sean John jeans that covered the top of her black Jordans. She also had a black leather European shoulder bag.

"Hey, bruh," I said and invited her in.

"Bruh? What the hell?" I heard her mumble. "So you're the famous Silk?" she said slyly and then stared me up and down before walking in. "You are kinda sexy if I say so my damn self. Yes, Lawd, Glory," she said sarcastically.

"Thanks, I think," I said in a surprised manner. "Take your shoes off and come on in. We were just playin' some pool downstairs. You play?" I heard Preacher mumble something else under her breath, but she refused to repeat it.

"Wait," she finally exclaimed as she placed her shoes neatly on the floor next to mine. "I gotta ask you something before you take me down to your little pit."

I was curious. What could she possibly want to ask me? "What is it?" I asked cautiously and waited for her response as I grabbed three beers from the fridge and a bag of Doritos.

"Look, I don't know much about you or what the hell this thing you and Timeka have going on here."

Preacher paused momentarily. I didn't know how to react. I was already nervous, but I refused to be disrespected in my own house - best friend or not.

"Listen, man, I got this," I assured her.

"I'm sure you do," Preacher interrupted. "Timeka is my best friend, but you, my friend, are a stranger and I don't trust you yet. Just tell me why--"

"What's going on up here? What's taking you guys so long?" Taz interrupted and came upstairs to join us. Taz smiled at both of us and then gave Preacher dap. "Is this where the party is?"

"Nooo," Preacher quickly said smiling. "I was just

telling Silk how much I like her artwork. Isn't it funny how the most beautiful picture can play tricks on your eyes?" Preacher said and looked back in my direction. I took a quick sip of beer, turned my head, and walked away.

"I guess," Taz responded and proceeded to briefly talk about some of the pictures on the wall. "So what do you guys want to do the rest of the day?"

I really wanted to stay and watch the football games, but I suggested we go to Pinz, a popular bowling alley in Midtown. It wasn't too far away and we could have a few beers and pizza. Taz was all for it, but Preacher wasn't, claiming she was trying to lose weight. She didn't appear to be in bad health. We were about the same height and weight, but her shoulders were much broader than mine, giving her the look of a more tapered upper body. Taz said Preacher worked out as much as we did and had a very solid, athletic build. I didn't know if she ever played the game before, but she looked like a football player.

   After a few minutes of discussion, we finally settled on Grandma's Garden, a homestyle soup and salad restaurant across town near the Onyx Megaplex. I was still worried about what Preacher wanted to ask me, but I refused to let it bother me too much. It made me feel good to see Taz so happy to have all of us together. I didn't know what to expect, but I was ready for just about anything.

# Preferences

*At that moment, it became clear. Femme pussy bored me. I didn't like the daintiness and softness of a woman who was too femme to really get down the way I liked it. I was turned on by the roughneck stud in a jersey, baggy pants, and a temp-fade with a killer jump shot.*

## Chapter 2

Lunch with Taz and Preacher wasn't as bad as I thought it would be, at least not at first. Preacher told me how she and Taz met and the fun things they used to do together. From there, all we could talk about was sports, especially the upcoming Steelers and Falcons game. Preacher was a die-hard Falcons fan, even back in the day when the team couldn't buy a winning season. It wasn't easy getting her to see how a weak offensive line was the

Falcons' Achilles' heel despite the fact the team got four of the best picks in the draft. In the end, I made a $100 bet against her Dirty Birds because I knew they couldn't handle the Steelers' defense, which was one of the best in the NFL. She accepted with extreme confidence.

Taz didn't want to go against the home team, but favored the Steelers. The Steelers was one of her favorite NFL teams despite its tragic win-loss record last season. Her argument was based on the Steelers' passing game and the Falcons' new running game. She even compared the two teams' ability to convert on third and fourth downs. With Taz, everything could be reasoned.

When it came to certain things, like sports, Taz was a true fence-rider. She always tried to find something good on each side, which made it difficult for her to choose one side over the other. That was frustrating for me at first. I liked people who could make a choice and stick with it. Somehow, Taz's inability to do that turned into one of the things that made her more attractive to

35

me. It made "us" seem more real.

Although Preacher and I seemed to hit it off quite well while Taz was around, there were moments I wasn't quite sure how to act or what to say. I felt Preacher was looking through me and was trying hard to find something wrong with me. She needed something that would give her leverage and I didn't know what that might have been. It made me uncomfortable, but I didn't want Taz to know.

"Well," Taz said as she stood up from the table and looked at both of us, "that strawberry lemonade is no joke. I'll be right back." There was a brief moment of silence and then it happened.

"So, what do you see in her?" Preacher asked boldly after Taz excused herself. We both watched as Taz headed down a long hallway toward the restroom at the back of the restaurant with her hands in her pockets.

"What do you mean by that?" I replied after my initial moment of shock. I took a quick sip of Sprite and anxiously waited for her reply.

"Look," Preacher said and resumed in a hushed voice, "we all know you're the man. I'm sure these horny ass femmes throw the pussy at you the minute you show your pearly whites and hit 'em with a little charm. You're like a Morris Chestnut with dreads." She hesitated then grinned sharply. "So what's up with you? Why Timeka?"

Preacher rubbed me the wrong way, but she had a point. I've had my share of tamed and untamed pussy. Most of the time, it was just handed to me. I didn't have to work for it at all. All I had to do was dial a number and before I could hang up the phone, some girl was at my door waiting for the chance to get a little action. Sometimes all I had to do was text 911 to a girl and she knew what was up.

Having the pussy tossed at me without effort became a waste of my time. There wasn't any more fun in having sex. Many of the girls I messed around with always expected something big, but didn't want to do anything for it. There just wasn't a good challenge and I enjoyed a good challenge.

My first time hopping in bed with someone who looked and acted like me was, at first, weird. I thought "how could I fuck this nigga?" I wanted a challenge and that's what I got. Her name was Jessie, but people called her Tank. She was someone who could take it as much as she dicked it out and someone I could still talk shit with over a game of basketball. At that moment, it became clear. I didn't like the daintiness and softness of a woman who was too femme to really get down the way I liked it. I was turned on by the roughneck stud in a jersey, baggy pants, and a temp-fade with a killer jump shot. I was turned on by the kind of stud who could just say fuck it and do what felt right. Taz wasn't that person at all. Somehow, I still fell for her.

"I'll give it to you, Silk. You got some serious ass swag. Your game is tight. So, why Timeka? I mean, dude, slappin' straps? That's gay as hell."

I tried to remain calm. It wasn't the first time I was in this position. "I know you don't understand me," I responded defensively, "and you don't have to. I'm not asking for your approval or your permission."

She seemed bothered by what I said. "Pump your brakes! It's not like that at all. I don't care what you do. I'm just lookin' out for my dawg."

"Why do you feel she needs to be looked out for anyway?" I asked sarcastically. "Whether you believe it or not, I love Taz and that's all to it."

"Your love ain't got shit to do with me." She paused momentarily and leaned in closer to speak. Her eyes were fixated on mine. "There's something about you that doesn't sit well with me. I think you're hiding something behind that pretty smile of yours. In fact, I know it. I saw the town's biggest freak, Zodiac, leave your crib with Reece. What was up with that?"

"That's none of your business," I exclaimed as I thought back to that night and how mad Taz was the next day. I had to tell Taz what was going on with Zodiac because she was determined and wouldn't let it go. I guess she never told Preacher about the situation and I wasn't dumb enough to do it either. That was a whole new conversation altogether and I wasn't about to get into it with her. That would be all the ammo she'd need to really cause problems for me.

"You can think that if you want to, playa," Preacher said. "Timeka is my business. I'm usually a good judge of character. Ask Timeka. I won't stop until I find out who you really are behind that pretty smile. Bruh."

The conversation ended in dead silence. The only words spoken came from the waitress, a beautiful Latina with long, dark hair named Maria. She asked if we needed anything else as she placed the check on the table between us. Preacher looked at me while Maria refilled her glass with unsweet tea. I waited patiently for a third round of Sprite. By the time Taz came back, the check was paid, and the tension between Preacher and me grew to an uncomfortable silence.

"What's up, guys?" Taz asked surprisingly. "That's the second time today you two have stopped talking when I come around. Is there something I should know about? What's up?"

"No, nothing's wrong. We're just getting to know each other," I said in an effort to maintain some peace and not alarm her to what was really happening.

"Yeah," Preacher followed along. "We're just trying to find out who we really are in this big old world."

After lunch, Taz and I settled on a quiet evening at her place. Alex and Taylor came over later in the evening and told us about all the fun they had. Taz and I watched the big games on television while the girls watched movies in the den. Later, we all hung out in the kitchen, cooked some spaghetti and garlic bread, which was my favorite meal, and played games.

# Passion

*She sighed and before long, all the unnecessary small talk and useless resistance stopped. I had her just where I wanted her, pinned on her back over the armrest wearing nothing but a smile and a look of satisfaction.*

## Chapter 3

I was really feeling Taz this morning. I watched from the living room as she moved about in the kitchen reading the back of an Aunt Jemima pancake box. She wasn't the best cook in the world, but it didn't matter. I definitely wanted breakfast, but not the kind she was cooking up. I was ready for some real action, especially after my little whatever that was with Preacher. What better way to release some energy than with a little morning sex?

Taz looked sexy in her blue checkerboard Polo pajamas and slippers. I could see the rings of carefully trained waves under her blue satin durag. The intoxicating scent of Giorgio that she put on around the nape of her neck and chest teased my senses and forced me to want to be near her. I continued to stare as she poured me a cup of coffee and set it on the end table next to me. I smiled then winked at her.

"What are you grinning about?" Taz asked as she sat down on the couch, removed her durag, and methodically brushed her hair. "What's on the agenda?"

"You," I replied.

She looked at me strangely. "As tempting as that sounds, we can't get into that right now."

She had a point. We had so much to do today. Christmas was just a few days away and like most people, we waited until the last minute to start shopping. It was our first Christmas together and I was really looking forward to it. It was the first time in a long time I had someone I loved, other than the girls, to spend time with during the holidays. Usually, I would buy the girls some weird-looking baby dolls with funny pink dresses and fruity lip glosses and spend the rest of my time at the movie theater. It was a tradition my sister and I started years ago after our dad died. But this year was different. This year, I wasn't alone and I had something to be happy about. This year, I had Taz.

"Baby," I pleaded with her in my usual way, hoping to turn her on with a quick eyebrow raise and mischievous smile.

"Baby, nothing! We have to go. You know I hate crowds, especially crowds of stupid people trying to buy stuff they know they can't afford."

She sipped the rest of her coffee, a blend of caramel and rich fudge topped with double whipped cream. All I could do was look at her and grin. I loved when she turned me down. Most times, it meant she wanted me to ignore what she said and force her to give in. This was one of those times, considering she never moved off the couch.

I was anxious and excited. I couldn't wait for her anymore. I took off my t-shirt and rubbed my abs. Then, I reached into my boxers and slowly stroked MD while she watched attentively. I looked in her eyes. She resisted my stare, but I knew she couldn't hold out forever. She never could. She wanted me.

"What are you doing?" Taz asked as if she didn't know what was about to happen.

"What does it look like?" I responded and stood directly in front of her, still stroking MD and looking into her eyes.

Taz suddenly became less anxious to shop. She leaned back on the leather couch and placed her coffee cup on the other end table. She slowly unbuttoned her shirt, showing those lean sculpted abs I couldn't get enough of, and clasped her hands behind her head. She stared at me as I kissed the faint line of hair just below her navel leading to the spot I couldn't wait to explore. I pulled her pants down and over her ankles, leaving her sitting on the couch with nothing but her black and red trimmed Polo boxers. I kissed her calves and slowly made my way up to her knees and inner thighs. I carefully slid my thumb across her clit until she was wet, which didn't take long at all.

"We have to go," Taz reminded me.

"We don't have to do a damn thing," I said boldly and spread her legs apart even more. "But one of us needs to chill out."

She looked surprised by what I said, but she knew I was serious. She grinned.

"I didn't stutter," I emphasized and then canvassed her clit with my tongue.

She sighed and before long, all the unnecessary small talk and useless resistance stopped. I had her just where I wanted her, pinned on her back over the armrest wearing nothing but a smile and a look of satisfaction.

I dragged her gently to the floor. I squeezed her breasts with one hand and put two fingers gently inside her. She could take more, but I wasn't ready to give it to her yet. I thrust my fingers in and out as she arched her back and called my name repeatedly. It was time. I gave her a third and then a fourth finger. My hand was drenched. She opened her legs wider and I knew she was ready for whatever I had to bring at that point.

"Fuck me!" She demanded.

I was more than willing to make it happen. I jerked her up in one solid motion and laid her down on the soft white carpet. I pushed her legs up so that her knees were just behind her shoulders, giving me all the room I needed to do my thing.

For the next few minutes, Taz and MD became even more acquainted. I penetrated deep inside her. Every stroke made her grab my lower back tighter and tighter. Every stroke made her body jerk a little more. When I thought she was close to climax, I turned her around, doggy style. She always liked that, at least that's what she told me. I held her by her waist with one hand and placed my other hand on her upper spine to push her body closer to the carpet. I gave everything I could to make sure she'd never forget me. My goal was to break her back and have her thank me for the privilege later.

After a while, all I heard was silence as Taz tried desperately to grab the carpet. I held steady because I wanted to share in her excitement as she came. Seconds later, she tried to hold back as she screamed my name. All I heard was a faint scream pierce its way through her lips. Her body shook as she reached for me to come closer. She finally relaxed and lay flat on the floor.

"I love you," Taz whispered and closed her eyes momentarily.

We spent the rest of the afternoon lying on the couch, drinking coffee, and watching *Sanford and Son* reruns on BET. Taz wanted more. She wanted to make me feel the same way, too, but I was content. I didn't need anything else. She looked at me with disappointment and turned her attention back to Fred and his witty insults against Aunt Esther. I rubbed Taz's feet until she eventually fell asleep. As she lay there in nothing but her socks and boxers, I sat on the couch, lit a Black and Mild, and thought about the look on Taz's face before she fell asleep.

Before me, Taz wasn't the type to let anyone handle her like I have. She wasn't one of those touch-me-not studs either because she'd saddle up in a heartbeat for some good head. I was the same way. I couldn't understand why most studs didn't like a woman to touch them. Even men got their dicks sucked so what made studs any different? That's the one thing that turned me off about a few people I was interested in back in the day.

That night when we had a threesome with Reece was the first time Taz had ever been with someone like me. It happened suddenly and I knew it threw her off. Even I was shocked, but I couldn't help it. Taz was smart, fine as hell, and I could really relate to her. She had a different kind of swag, one I couldn't resist.

I continued to stare at Taz as she changed positions and lay her head in my lap. I hoped she knew how much I loved her. I hoped I wasn't just something to satisfy her curiosity.

# Family

*I looked forward to a moment like this where her life and independence was in my hands for a change. But that wasn't my life anymore. However, I was always willing to make exceptions for my family.*

## Chapter 4

It was almost Christmas and I was very excited. I convinced Taz to stay home with the girls while I managed the crowds at the Onyx Megaplex. Shopping was never one of Taz's favorite things to do around this time of year, so I knew she wouldn't mind keeping the girls occupied. We already bought them baby dolls, Dora books, clothes, and a bicycle for each of them. Today was my day to shop for Taz.

I was on the grind. I hit up Distinguished

Gentlemen and Armani Exchange for Taz a new suit and shoes and Cartman Jewelers for a new TAG Heuer watch. Along the way, I picked up a few other things I thought Taz might enjoy like the new Maxwell CD and a bottle of John Varvatos cologne. Before I knew it, it was already 5:30 and I was starved. I figured I could grab a quick snack and then take my family out to dinner at the new Italian restaurant around the corner.

I made my way to the food court. The smell of fresh-baked pretzels from Sue's Twists, chocolate chip cookies at Mike's, New York style pizza, grilled burgers, bourbon chicken, and sweet cinnamon rolls called out to me all at once. To make things easy for myself, I settled for a chicken nuggets kids' meal at Chick-Fil-A and sat at a small, quiet table near the escalators overlooking the lower level.

It was so crowded in the mall. I could understand why Taz hated shopping during the holidays. People were always in a rush and never paid attention to where they were going. Those who weren't in a hurry lazily walked

53

around window shopping taking up space and wasting everyone else's time. Old men in denim overalls and red plaid shirts were stuck sitting on uncomfortable wooden benches waiting for their family members to remember where they left them. Kids raced wildly down the aisles on those annoying rollerskate sneakers. Sales geeks pushed every product there was and parking was a real bitch. It was temporary anarchy to say the least.

I had just completed the crossword puzzle on the Chick-Fil-A bag and put together the toy airplane that was inside when something caught my attention. I was shocked by who I saw riding slowly up the escalators wearing all black. It was Dominic. I was paralyzed. I dropped my Sprite on the floor, spilling some of it and crushed ice on my bags. I turned my head hoping she wouldn't see me. I wasn't in the mood for bullshit and drama today, especially with her.

I had to admit Dominic was still sexy. She had smooth, caramel skin, full lips, dark, curly hair that she always kept in a ponytail, and a strong New Jersey accent.

Her smile could charm the panties off anybody. Straight women found themselves wanting a taste of "Nic's dick." Dominic was quiet most times, but explosive when it came to money and sex. She and Taz were nothing alike and for that, I was thankful.

Dominic and I met years ago when she lived in the same projects as my sister. We somehow picked each other's card and started secretly seeing each other. Things were good. Before long, though, she was caught up in the thug life around her and the thrill that came with thinking she was the shit. She joined a gang and eventually, so did I. The last time I heard anything about her, she was serving time in a Mississippi prison for assaulting a police officer, drug trafficking, and money laundering. Taz never knew about Dominic or my old gang days and I planned on keeping it that way. It may not have been the best move to make, but it was my only option.

Dominic was just about to walk off the last step while I struggled to grab my stuff and leave. I didn't want a confrontation, but it was too late. Anxiety caused my delay and I was forced to engage.

"My nigga, Silk!" Dominic exclaimed and offered me dap, which I refused. "What's the deal, man?"

"I should be asking you the same thing," I said harshly. "Your deal was ten to twenty. Or, am I mistaken?"

"Now is that any kinda way to treat an old friend? I thought your mama raised you better than that?"

I remained as calm as I could. I was very protective of my mother and sister, even in death. But I refused to relive my old boxing days and give in to temptation and punch Dominic in the mouth.

"Why are you here? What do you want?" I asked.

"Can a nigga shop like all these other merry bastards around here? I got folks I love and shit, too." She paused and looked down at my bags. "You always had good taste, my nigga? Cartman's, huh? You 'bout to Beyoncé some bitch in the ATL? No, wait," she said, laughed, and leaned in closer to me. "Two niggas can't get hitched in the South. You gotta go to the fuckin'

56

president's backyard for that shit, huh?"

I looked her in the eyes and remained silent. She was the type to definitely start shit, but I was the type to finish it if I had to. At that moment all I could think about was what she wanted. Why was she not in jail? Why was she here? Was this coincidence or another trick by Zodiac?

Until recently, I did everything Zodiac wanted me to do. I was with every undercover lesbian there was who just wanted to satisfy their curiosity from Bankhead to Buckhead all the way to the sticks of South Georgia. I went with every group of bachelorettes who wanted to get their last quick fix before saying "I do." From basketball players and teachers to the pricks in politics, I did my duty and I did it well. I avoided putting my mouth on any of them, especially since all they really wanted was MD. I even hung out with guys who just wanted to know how to make their woman come harder. At times, it seemed Taz had enough of sharing me with strangers. I had to convince her it was just business, an evening guaranteed to turn $4,000 or more. Most importantly, it helped keep Zodiac off my back.

Lately, Zodiac's been quiet. There were no calls or late night appointments in the past couple months. I figured I was done. Still, something wasn't right. If all was straight, Dominic wouldn't be standing in front of me. So, there had to be a catch. I was curious.

"Why the hell are you here, Nic?"

"Like I said, I'm here to shop," she said and sat down at the table. She looked up and smiled. "Why don't you join me?"

"I'm busy."

"I asked nicely. Now I'm tellin' you. Sit your Brokeback Mountain ass down!"

In no time at all, an entourage of studs with long ponytails dressed in leather coats and jeans surrounded me. I laughed to hide my nervousness. I should have known Dominic wasn't alone. I sat down reluctantly while the rest of her crew sat at a nearby table with their eyes fixed on me. We were in the middle of a crowded mall and yet, I felt alone and helpless. Even so, I was ready.

"What's this all about, Nic? You got some kind of beef with me?"

"Now I'm insulted by that. I told you I'm just out shopping. But since you asked, there is one thing."

My heart started racing. I became more and more convinced that whatever was going on had Zodiac's name all over it. It was her style to let others do the stuff she didn't want to do on her own.

"I know about you and your little attorney friend. Timeka, right? She's cute," she said under her breath.

I was filled with rage. "What do you want?"

"I don't know how to say this," she said. "It's never been my thing, but I'm sorry."

"Sorry?"

"Sorry I got dirt on your beautiful, white carpet. I don't know where my manners were. Relax," Dominic said. "The girls and your little boy-toy are fine. At least they'll be fine as long as you behave."

I stood up quickly, grabbed Dominic by the

collar, and leaned her over the wall of the food court. Her hat fell slowly to the floor below next to a group of young teenage girls who were pointing our way. Her buddies stood up quickly to get to me, but she signaled for them to chill. All of the things she and I went through flashed across my eyes. The time we spent robbing people, selling high-end drugs, and violence gave me reason to drop her onto the lower level and be satisfied. I looked forward to a moment like this where her life and independence was in my hands for a change. But that wasn't my life anymore. However, I was always willing to make exceptions for my family.

"Nigga, don't do me," I exclaimed. "If you go anywhere near my girls or Taz again, I promise you it'll be the last time you ever draw breath again. They'll be finding pieces of your ass scattered across the Chattahoochee. I will fucking kill you, Nic! You feel me, dawg?"

I backed off and let her go as swarms of nosy people with camera phones walked by to get a closer look at what was going on. Dominic used to intimidate me and

I felt I had to give in to whatever she wanted, but not this time. I had more to lose now and I was willing to protect it at all costs, even if it meant my own freedom.

"You always had balls, Silk. That's one thing I admired about you," Dominic said as she grinned and straightened her jacket and sweater. "It was quite a turn on actually."

I grabbed the rest of my bags and started to walk away just as two muscular mall security guards stood between us.

"Is there a problem here, fellas?" one of the guards asked.

"No, officer," Nic replied. "My friend and I just had a disagreement."

I looked at each of Dominic's friends as I walked away to let them know I wasn't scared of them either. As I turned the corner to walk toward the escalator, Dominic yelled.

"Check your mail." Dominic said and stared at me as I walked away. "One love, baby."

# The South

*Tuesday was Youth Night. Wednesday was Bible Study. Thursday was choir rehearsal. Friday was prayer night. Saturday was Community Service Day. It was a must for them to be at the 9AM and 1PM worship services on Sunday. Aside from all that, they were just average kids, but with an old folks spirit.*

## Chapter 5

Christmas morning had come and gone. Alex and Taylor quickly opened their gifts, scattered red and silver holiday wrapping paper and gift tissue all over the living room, and rode their new pink bicycles around the neighborhood all afternoon. The next day, I watched from the front steps as pink ribbons from their handlebars rippled wildly in the wind. The girls seemed so happy. I couldn't help being proud of them for being not just good kids, but smart kids. Just the other day, Alex was already talking about college at MIT while Taylor, our very own

CSI mini-cop, had her sights set on being an FBI agent.

As I sat and watched them ride their bikes with the neighborhood kids, I thought about how things could have been for them. Even though they both had book smarts, Alex and Taylor were no strangers to the knowledge that came from some of life's most challenging, harsh realities. Growing up in the projects, they saw things I never wanted them to see. They understood things most kids their age wouldn't have a clue about. They were tough and gentle at the same time. Maybe it had something to do with how they were raised or the fact Debbie had them in church all the time. Tuesday was Youth Night. Wednesday was Bible Study. Thursday was choir rehearsal. Friday was prayer night. Saturday was Community Service Day. It was a must for them to be at the 9AM and 1PM worship services on Sunday. Aside from all that, they were just average kids, but with an old folks spirit.

Christmas morning for the girls was exciting, but Taz was a different story. She opened every gift with a fake look of surprise. I guess all the hints she gave since late September were supposed to guarantee I got what she wanted. As she opened her gifts, I loved seeing the smile on her face. It was more satisfying than anything she could have given me, even though I wasn't complaining at all.

When I saw a small, blue box with a silver bow on top under the tree, I thought it must have been the diamond cuff links I was looking at a few weeks ago. In the back of my mind, I was hoping there was something more than just that one box because it was the only one from her that had my name on it. She surprised me. Inside the box was a tiny black key on a leather keychain. She walked me over to the garage. When I saw a blue and white Yamaha Sport motorcycle with silver trim, all I could do was scream with joy and imagine myself on the open road in blue denim and black leather with a bold helmet that read "Smooth Rider."

Before long, an uneasy feeling crept in and replaced my vision of an open road with thoughts of despair and anxiety. The incident between Dominic and me at the mall weighed heavy on my mind. I found the letter she left for me in the mailbox under some junk mail. I put the letter in my back pocket until I had time to read it. I was anxious to see what kind of bullshit Dominic had in mind. It simply read:

*What's up, Silk? I see you're a real family man now. That's cool. You're probably wondering why in the hell I'm here and how the fuck I found you. It's not important. You know me. Life's changed since the hood. I roll different, but I stay connected. One thing I know is this. Your boy toy is trouble. I don't need somebody snoopin' around my hood and askin' my folks shit. You and I both know suits don't stand a chance in the hood. You and me may have had beef back in the day, but I still got mad love for you. But don't test me. A threat to what's mine is personal. Keep your lil' nigga outta Chucktown.*      *-- Diamond D*

I was beyond surprised. I didn't know what to think. I thought all the secrets between Taz and me were out, at least the ones that really mattered. I was confused and curious. Why would Taz be in South Carolina and when did she have time to go with her workload? What was she hiding and why? What did Nic have to do with it? Then, curiosity turned into anger. Even the gentle morning breeze was not enough to bring peace and solitude as it had for so many months. As the blue sky gave way to dark clouds and raindrops, I made up my mind. I was going to confront Taz as soon as possible.

# Revelations

*Zodiac's plan was to connect herself in Charleston then bring the business to Atlanta, the one place where she knew there'd be a huge clientele. After all, Atlanta was the Hollywood of the South. With so many athletes, entertainers, actors, and businesspeople in one place, she could generate millions and go unnoticed.*

## Chapter 6

"You'll never guess what happened today," Taz said enthusiastically as we watched the 6 o'clock news on Channel 9 at Taz's house.

I had no idea what Taz was about to say. She seemed excited and I didn't want to interrupt her flow.

"Guess who called today and said she wanted me to be her agent?"

"Who?" I asked.

"Alicia Johnson! You know, AJ?"

I knew AJ very well. We played basketball together for a while in college and for about a year overseas. She was a point guard and she had major skills. She even gave me a run for my money a few times and I've always been at the top of my game. The last time we saw each other was at a 3 on 3 charity basketball tournament in Ireland. Our team lost, but we still celebrated big time at one of Ireland's famous pubs.

Off the court, AJ was bad. She was beautiful with long, brown hair, caramel skin, full lips, and had dimples that complimented her perfect smile. She was down to earth and didn't get into a lot of the drama most of our teammates found themselves in. People always assumed we were a couple. We played along because it seemed normal, but I knew her secrets and she knew most of mine.

"That's great, Taz!" I exclaimed. "She's one of the hottest players out there. But isn't AJ still on contract overseas?"

"Yeah, and that's the beauty of it. Her contract

will be up soon and she'll be a free agent. There's a new team in South Carolina that wants to pick her up before the Atlanta Dream gets a chance to make an offer."

"South Carolina?" I asked with some hesitation.

I knew the South Carolina Cougars had a good team. I saw them practice a few times in the old Panther Stadium last summer. If they picked up AJ, they had a good chance of at least making it to the playoffs their first season. There was something still bothering me, though. South Carolina really stood out in my head and it had nothing at all to do with AJ.

"So, you have to go up there?" I asked and changed the channel to something less depressing while Taz fumbled through her briefcase of papers, fine pens, and calendars.

"Maybe," she replied.

"When was the last time you were in South Carolina?"

Opportunity knocked with a sense of purpose as I talked. AJ's contract was the perfect segway into South

Carolina without me having to think too much about Taz's intentions or mention Dominic's letter. My question seemed subtle, but it was loaded with doubts, anxiety, and suspicion.

"It's been a while, probably three years ago. I was there for our family reunion," she replied.

Like all other attorneys, Taz seemed very convincing. Her demeanor never changed and her attention stayed focused on the stack of papers and bright yellow legal pad she pulled out and placed on her lap.

"So, when will you know if you have to go?" I asked impatiently. "Why would you have to go there anyway?

Taz seemed frustrated. "What's up with the million and eighteen questions? I feel like I'm the one on trial."

In a way, Taz was on trial. I needed to know what business she had that was so important, Dominic had to find me. I was uncomfortable not knowing the situation and scared of what the truth may have been. I was happy about AJ, which was a huge deal if Taz could pull off a big contract. But, I knew there was more. I knew there was something she wasn't telling me.

"I gotta ask you something and I want the hard ass truth." I turned the television off, placed Taz's stack of papers on the coffee table, and continued. She was puzzled and gave me a confusing stare. "Have you been in South Carolina in the last few months?"

"Weren't you listening?" she replied. "It's been years."

My tone became a little more stern and direct. I could tell she was trying hard to keep her composure. She leaned back on the couch and tried to grab the remote from my hands. She mumbled something under her breath, but chose not to repeat it. I went in because she wasn't giving me what I wanted.

"Someone told me you've been snooping around in Chucktown lately? Is that true?"

"First off, tell your buddies to mind their own business. If I had been anywhere near Chucktown, don't you think I'd tell you?"

"No," I quickly responded before she had a chance to start again. "Not if you were in some kind of trouble. Don't bullshit me, Taz. I hate that."

She remained silent for what seemed like an hour as she hung her head and massaged the back of her neck. She looked at me briefly and then turned her attention to a squirrel posted by a tree in the front yard. All of a sudden, her frustration and the secrets she kept came rushing out. I didn't know if I should be worried or relieved, happy or sad, or if I should start watching my back and Taz's.

"Remember that night you had one of your so-called appointments? I told you I was hangin' with Preacher at The Flame just to relax. That wasn't completely true." She paused for a moment, took a deep breath, and continued. "I went there to talk to Zodiac. Preacher just happened to show up."

I was pissed, especially after I heard the name, Zodiac. "Why the fuck did you do that? I told you Zodiac

74

is a crazy ass bitch!"

"I'm not afraid of her!" Taz yelled and stood up and walked over to the window. She's nothin', you hear me? Nothin'!"

"I always thought you were smart, Taz, but have you lost your fuckin' mind?" I asked. "What did you have to say to her? I told you to stay away from her."

"Silk, I'm grown! I don't need your permission to talk to anybody! But since you asked, I'll tell you what happened."

I found out more than I really wanted. Taz had been to Charleston a few times. On the days she was supposed to be at the office, she was trying to get dirt on Zodiac. She thought she was helping me get out the game and keep the girls safe. During one of her little trips, she discovered some very interesting information that could leave Zodiac in deep with a lot of people.

"Let's just say she's not who she says she is and all this extra fuckin' you've been doing could be over. You can thank me later," Taz said in a loud, angry voice.

It was unusual for Taz to cuss, even when the situation called for it. She was always reserved, cordial, and ahead of the game. It was a sexy look for her even when I was pissed off with her. I held back a grin as she put her glasses on and reached for the stack of papers I took from her. I figured she was testing me since she knew I hated when we were talking about something serious and I didn't have her undivided attention. Test or not, I wasn't going to fall for it. I needed answers and my patience was almost gone.

"Thank you for what? Are you serious? What have you done? I got people tellin' me they're gonna fuck you up because you don't know how to mind your own business. Even after I told you to leave that bitch alone. Wait on a thank you! Better yet, thank me when I stop those niggas from puttin' a bullet in your ass."

"You ungrateful mother--! I'm trying to help you out!" Taz stopped just shy of what she really wanted to say. "Look, you're right! I should've just chilled, but I couldn't miss out on this. I needed all of you and watching you get all trump-tight for somebody else was pissin' me the fuck off."

A few minutes went by before we could talk to one another. On the one hand, I was feeling some kind of way because we just had our first real argument. On the flip side, this was serious.

After we both calmed down, Taz told me all the details. Although she had family in Dallas, New York, and Denver, Zodiac had a very special connection in Charleston. Like me, she was living a double life. She fooled everybody, even me. For years, I knew her only as Zodiac, the one who was making my life miserable. Thanks to Taz, I now know Zodiac as Brandon.

It was in Charleston that Brandon was actually running the show. He was smart and had a business mind. Unfortunately, that business mind was wasted on the streets. Brandon hated being "Brandon," so he figured out a way to do something about it. After a lot of planning and hustling, he put together a rather elegant escort and drug business. That business funded his transition to become Zodiac, the person I despised the most, and it helped fund the lifestyle I have now. Zodiac's plan was to connect herself in Charleston then bring the business to Atlanta, the one place where she knew there'd be a huge clientele. After all, Atlanta was the Hollywood of the South. With so many athletes, entertainers, actors, and businesspeople in one place, she could generate millions and go unnoticed.

What people didn't know about Zodiac was that she was in deep with the wrong people in Charleston and Atlanta. If they found out who she really was, it'd be lights out for her. I wouldn't be sad about it either. She deserved whatever happened to her.

# Wisdom

*"It's not my place to judge you. That's God's work. But if you're going to be whatever God intended you to be, be classy with it. Be a lady. Keep your stuff decent and in order!"*

## Chapter 7

    Taz and I spent the morning cutting the grass, trimming hedges, and power-washing both of our houses. Even though it was late Winter, it was unusually warm outside. We both put on a tank top, basketball shorts, and an old pair of Nike's. The sun was beating down on us as sweat rolled down our arms and back. I lit my second Black and Mild, drenched Taz with the water hose, and kept going. Between the two of us, we got the lawns done in no time. The last thing we did was wash the cars. My old 2000 Nissan hadn't had a wash in a month at least. Taz was more attentive with her ride, a 2008 Limited Edition Ford F150 Super Cab truck she called "Max."

Max was bright red with black leather interior, 22-inch Gitano chrome rims, chrome trim, factory-tinted dark windows, and had a license plate that read, "MAYIHLPU. It was equipped with the latest GPS and radar tracking system, BOSE speakers with an HD satellite radio, voice-operated everything, and the weirdest alarm system I've ever seen. Max wouldn't start unless Taz said, "Hello, Max," and even then there was some kind of voice recognition chip that validated the startup. It was all too much for me, but I guess it was standard equipment for a big shot attorney like Taz.

I couldn't get into cars like Taz, even though I had the money to do whatever I wanted to do. While my associates were out buying 7-series Benzes, diamond rings, and hanging out at the strip clubs every weekend, I was busy doing other things. I saved a lot of money while playing basketball overseas plus I still had money left over from my mom's life insurance. Unfortunately, I still had Zodiac to thank for some of my cash flow. When I closed the deal on the house next to Taz, I didn't need a mortgage. I talked with the realtor, negotiated a deal with the seller, and then walked into closing with a guaranteed check for $200,000. It was my first home and it was all mine.

I finished washing my car in about ten minutes. Taz was still making love to Max with a special shampoo and singing some old Gerald Levert song. As she made her way around to clean the tires, I thought about what happened a few days earlier. At first, it was hard for me to understand Taz's intentions. All I could think about was how could she put herself in harm's way. She had to be crazy. Then again, maybe that was all the confirmation I needed to know for sure that our relationship wasn't just a passing fad for her. It was real. If it took all of that for her to protect me, surely I could do the same thing. It was only right.

I was still pissed off, though. What did Nic have

to do with anything? Why was it such a big deal that Taz was asking about Zodiac? I laughed and thought maybe Zodiac and Nic were bedroom buddies at some point. Then again, Reece has been in the picture, too. I thought it was strange that she came over my house with Zodiac. That was the same night Taz had Blackjack Night with her friends and didn't invite me. Reece slipped up and said something that night that was off the wall, but I just let it go as lesbian drama and forgot all about it until now. It had something to do with spending time with Zodiac at some clinic in Aiken, South Carolina. Whatever the situation, I knew I'd have to figure it out, for my sake and T'az's.

As I sat on the porch waiting for Taz to be done, something caught my attention. It was Mrs. Carter. She was standing in her doorway wearing that same old flowered robe she wore all the time. She was looking right at us, but didn't say a word. I felt like I was caught up in some horror movie and the bad guy was just waiting to pounce on me.

"Hey, what do you think is her problem?" I asked Taz as she rinsed Max.

"Who knows?" she replied. "I told you something wasn't right with that old lady."

"She's just not the talking kind," I joked. "She doesn't seem as bad as you make her out to be."

"Then maybe you can explain why she stares at us all the time. She never speaks. If you wave "hello" at her, she's likely to give you the bird. Yeah, she's the perfect neighbor," Taz said sarcastically.

I listened attentively as Taz cracked on Mrs. Carter. Mrs. Carter finally opened the screen door, stepped outside, held up a glass of iced tea, and motioned us to come over. Taz and I looked at each other in disbelief. Taz thought it was some kind of trick, but I talked her into going. We walked slowly across the street, stood on the porch, and waited for Mrs. Carter to invite us in.

"Well, are you coming in or what?" Mrs. Carter

asked.

We opened the screen door and slowly walked in. Mrs. Carter was standing in the kitchen. There was a strange odor that hit me so hard, I almost walked out. It smelled like peaches, peppermint, and Bengay cream. I looked around and saw little porcelain unicorns, ballet girls, and dolphins above the fireplace. There was a large, wooden bookcase that stretched an entire wall and it was full of books, magazines, and old newspapers. It was warm and humid outside, but even more so in Mrs. Carter's house.

"Sit down," Mrs. Carter said as she brought us iced tea and a tray of shortbread cookies.

"Are we supposed to sit on that?" I whispered to Taz.

I couldn't help it. The large sofa she wanted us to sit on had bright pink flowered prints and had a large, thick piece of plastic covering it. As we sat down, I just knew my legs were going to catch on fire. Thankfully, all of the family pictures on the wall helped take my attention off that.

"Quit trippin," Taz told me and then thanked Mrs. Carter.

"Mrs. Carter, it's nice of you to invite us over," Taz said as she grabbed cookies off the tray. "It sure is hot outside."

"I know," she replied.

There was a long, awkward silence. Mrs. Carter looked at us, but didn't say a thing. Taz and I just sat on the hot plastic sofa and admired all of the pictures on the wall. Some of them were black and white pictures of street signs, abandoned buildings, and vintage cars. There was an old newspaper hung in a black display frame. The year was 1935 and the headline read: "Depression Hits Farmers." Another framed newspaper read: "King Assassinated!" On the coffee table was an old, large-print Bible with tattered pages and a bunch of old JET and National Geographic magazines.

"So, Mrs. Carter," Taz said hesitantly. "Why did you invite us over?"

Taz went in and rightfully so. Mrs. Carter never invited us over before and never spoke to us. She was friendly with the girls, but with us, it was a different story. She always stared at us in a mean way and turned her nose up all the time. I just knew she hated us, but thought she was too dignified to admit it.

"Babies, I've been around a long time," Mrs. Carter said in a raspy voice. "I've seen things only your grandmamas could tell you about. I've been all over this world."

As she talked, all I could think about was playing basketball and a game of 9-ball. Mrs. Carter was an old lady and like most old ladies, she had a story to tell about everything. I wasn't sure what that story was, but it was about to be told right now. In my mind, I sighed and prepared myself for a journey back in time.

"What's the matter with you ladies?" Mrs. Carter asked.

"What do you mean, Mrs. Carter?" Taz asked. "Nothing's wrong."

"You know what I mean," she said confidently and took a big sip of her tea. "I know you're dykin' and if you like it, babies, I love it!"

Mrs. Carter was silent and so were we. She leaned back in her rugged, black leather recliner and relaxed. We were too afraid to get up and too afraid to stay. Then, things took a new direction.

"It's not my place to judge you. That's God's work. But if you're going to be whatever God intended you to be, be classy with it. Be a lady. Keep your stuff decent and in order!"

"Thanks, Mrs. Carter for the tea and cookies," Taz said politely as she stood up and placed her glass on the table. "It's getting late."

"I did not dismiss you. Until I do, you will sit and show me the respect I know you're more than capable of providing."

Mrs. Carter spoke with authority. Her blue eyes were wide open as she brushed back gray hair from her forehead. She stared at us. Because my momma would turn over in her grave three times if I moved, I sat there and convinced Taz to stay.

"But Mrs. Carter--" Taz said.

"Look, we've been neighbors a long time, Timeka, and I know you just moved here a few months ago, Sonya. Please, call me Mrs. C.," she said. "Mrs. Carter makes me feel old and I have a whole lot more livin' to do."

She stood up to show us some pictures in a dusty, brown photo album. Before she sat back down, Mrs. Carter glanced at an old picture on the wall. It was a black and white photo of her and a young man.

"I was married forty-two beautiful years until the Lord called my Sam home. He was a fine man. He was handsome, gentle, and strong. Everyone called him Pops, even me. We have five children, eight grandchildren, and two great-grandchildren."

I wasn't sure where any of this was going. I figured it was one of those old gay-bashing lectures with a side of tea, cookies, and a history lesson. I looked through the photo album as she talked and kept quiet. Taz faked being interested long enough to keep Mrs. Carter off our back. She kept talking about Sam, how they met, their children, and the things they used to get into.

"Mrs. C," Taz interrupted. "Who is this woman?"

Taz pointed to a picture of a beautiful young woman, around twenty or so, in a dress and sandals on the beach. I had to look twice myself. The girl looked familiar. Mrs. Carter looked at the photo, smiled, but didn't respond.

"Yes, I loved Sam, but Sam had his own life and so did I," Mrs. Carter said and continued to ignore Taz's question. We just looked at each other and back at the photo, hoping Mrs. Carter would hurry things along.

"We had our ups and downs, but the ups kept us together. We saw things only you two could read about in the history books." Mrs. Carter smiled. Soon, her smile became a look of concern. "You see, Sam was my husband, but he was a man's man. And I was a lady's lady."

"Mrs. C., I don't understand," Taz said.

"It was a different time, Timeka. Sam and I loved each other, but our hearts were somewhere else. We entertained in our own special way. Friday nights were Sam's poker nights and Thursdays were my recipe nights. For Sam, five card stud meant spending private, intimate time with his male friends and for me, it meant sharing a lot more than a casserole or cake recipe."

We listened in disbelief as Mrs. Carter told us about how she and Sam would put up fronts with their friends and coworkers. They both worked at an engineering firm for years. Sam was a Project Manager and she was a Leadership Coach. Their marriage was good, but it only hid what they really wanted. On the surface, they were professionals with the perfect family. But like all families, they had skeletons.

"What I'm trying to say to you both is don't put what you do on the streets," Mrs. Carter said in a quiet voice. "The streets are for whores, hustlers, and pimps. The same care you give those girls is the same care you should have for your reputation. Sam and I learned from our mistakes. Don't go home to glory before correcting yours."

She drew me in and I felt like I was back home with Mama telling me all kinds of little stories and lessons about everything. Suddenly, the hot plastic and sweet smells didn't matter as much. I smiled and listened attentively. I had a newfound respect for her.

"The young lady in the picture is my granddaughter, Zyon. In a lot of ways, I feel at fault for what happened to her. She was the victim of a lot of bad choices that I made. I'd give anything to take them back."

Mrs. Carter's face went blank. She looked sad. For the rest of the afternoon, Taz and I sat with Mrs. Carter. She told us about her childhood, living through the Martin years, and what it was like working at one of the nation's top engineering firms. After a while, she cheered up, fixed us another glass of tea, and brought out more cookies.

Almost every Sunday after that day, Taz, the girls, and I had Sunday dinner with Mrs. C. We all looked forward to it. I quickly locked in to my favorite meal at

Mrs. C.'s - yams, homemade mac and cheese, fried chicken, collard greens, and some old fashioned sweet tea. She'd always make some kind of pie or cake for dessert. Taz and I always had seconds. I missed my Mama's cooking, but Mrs. C's keepin' it old school without worrying about the calories cooking was a delicious substitute. It was weeks later that I learned the sweet smells coming from the kitchen were nothing more than peach and apple preserves, the perfect topping for the perfect homemade, Southern biscuit.

# Hail Mary

*If I rolled over in the middle of the night and told her to strap up,
Nic was the roughneck stud who could handle me the way I liked.
Even if I just asked her to…chill on the couch in a pair of boxers, a
tank top, and a baseball cap…If it had anything to do with sex,
Nic was ready. There were no limits, no boundaries, and no rules.*

## Chapter 8

Life was definitely different in Twin Oaks. The girls were growing up faster than I could keep up with them and making new friends everywhere they went. I was happy that I didn't have any new business, which gave me more time to relax. I seriously considered going back into the ring. I missed the action and no holds-barred fighting and getting paid for it. Their names were all different, but each opponent represented some challenge in my life. I figured that if I couldn't overcome them in real life, the squared circle was the next big thing.

I even grew fonder of Mrs. Carter. She was no longer the mean witch we thought she was. In fact, I looked forward to Sunday dinners at her house and hearing about the things she went through growing up in 1940s Mississippi. She didn't live far from my hometown of Cedartown, the home of Klan thugs, rednecks, and Bible-toting fanatics who thought they were at the right hand of God. She was used to the angry stares and somebody calling her "nigger." But in my neighborhood, I had to fight just to prove myself to anybody who didn't like me for whatever reason. I was triple-cursed and living in a town that hated me just because they could. I never started trouble, but somehow it always found me.

Things were different with me and Taz, too. We didn't play as much basketball or shoot as much pool as we used to, which surprised me. Taz thought she was twenty feet tall whenever she beat me in a game of 9-ball. She talked shit every chance she got. Now, it didn't seem to interest her too much anymore. It seemed like an inconvenience. At times, she was distant and cold. When I felt like a little action, she always gave me some kind of dumb excuse. I heard everything from headaches and Aunt Flow to she just had a lot of work to do. Most of the time, she'd say something about AJ and how she was trying hard to get the deal wrapped up. I was excited for her at first, but lately, something didn't feel right. I couldn't narrow it down to a single thing, so I didn't know how to react. I tried to play it safe and hope things would get better. In my mind, she was just busy being busy and not making anything happen.

Despite Taz's so-called busy schedule and lame excuses, I still had needs. I needed to be with her, back in our own world and away from all the bullshit and drama. I was frustrated, angry, and tired. I needed to unwind, especially since Christmas night was the last time I really put it down the way I wanted to.

I had a lot on my mind, especially Nic and our

run-in at the mall. I was pissed for a while, but then I started thinking about how we used to get down.

Sex was the one thing I could depend on Nic for regardless of what mood she was in or how much we argued. If I wanted her to give me some head in the kitchen right after breakfast and a cup of coffee, Nic was on it. If I rolled over in  the middle of the night and told her to strap up, Nic was the roughneck stud who could really handle me the way I liked. Even if I just asked her to light me a vanilla Black and Mild and chill on the couch in a pair of boxers, a tank top, and a baseball cap and touch herself, she was down. If it had anything to do with sex, Nic was ready. There were no limitations.

With Taz, however, things were different. I was tired of hearing "no" and "I'm busy." All I wanted to hear her say was "Yes, Sir" and "Daddy." I had all I could take and refused to sit around another night waiting for the mood to finally hit her. Whether she was feeling it or not, it was going down tonight. I called Taz to see what plans she had for tonight so I could quickly make them go away. She answered the phone reluctantly.

"What's wrong with you?" I asked.

"Nothing," she replied dryly and remained silent for the next few seconds.

"It doesn't sound like nothing," I commented.

"I'm fine."

I knew something was wrong. Her tone was very sad and melancholy, but I didn't push it. I knew she'd eventually tell me.

"I lost the contract," Taz said sadly. "AJ decided to go with a different agent, which leaves me back at square one."

"Wow, I'm sorry to hear that," I replied. "Is there anything you need?"

I tried to sound as sympathetic as I could, but in a way, I was glad Taz lost the contract. I had a strange feeling that something wasn't right about that whole thing, but I couldn't pull it all together. Maybe I didn't want to know.

"Yeah, another AJ," she said and attempted to laugh. "I'm gonna chill at home tonight. You can come by and watch the football game with me if you want. I just want to relax."

"Okay. I'll see you later," I assured her.

I wanted to cheer her up a little and make her forget about AJ, at least temporarily. I hung up the phone and ran upstairs to grab Taz's spare house key, which she left in my sock drawer a few months ago. Taz said she had a few stops to make and would be home in a couple of hours. I called, Kim, our baby-sitter, to see if she would be available tonight. The girls loved her and said they always have fun. Once the arrangements were made, I was off to Taz's house.

I made my entry and went straight to Taz's bedroom with a small box of goodies I had been holding on to ever since she became this super busy attorney. I placed the box on her bed, a California King with a custom made mahogany headboard she had delivered from a store in Texas. I looked around the bedroom to try to plan my attack.

Taz was very anal, so everything in her bedroom had its own place. She had a closet just for sneakers and dress shoes. Each time I opened that closet, it seemed there was a new pair of Stacy Adams, Comey's, Prada, or some other name brand. I didn't mind too much. Shoes weren't my thing anyway. I preferred tailored suits and ties in every color imaginable as long as they made me stand out and they attracted the right kind of attention.

Taz had a large dresser in her bedroom. It had eight spacious drawers and each one contained something different. One drawer was full of plain white t-shirts and a second drawer was reserved for nothing but blue and gray t-shirts. Another drawer contained dress socks. She even had a drawer full of different colored hankies that matched whatever she decided to wear.

I kept looking around until I came across what Taz called Treasure Island, a locked box that looked like some sort of lost treasure from *Pirates of the Caribbean*. Taz kept all kinds of things in that chest, some things she couldn't even show me. She had DVDs of men having sex with one another, magazines, Doc Johnsons of all sizes, vibrating bullets and rabbits, ticklers, lotions, massage oils, flavored condoms, anal beads, and a lot of other things. Before I became too distracted by everything Taz could do with those things, I walked past the chest and started setting the stage for a night of fun and relaxation.

I grabbed Taz's favorite pair of blue, plaid pajamas and laid them across the bed along with her special brush and durag. I turned the ceiling fan on high so the bedroom would be cool, but not too cold. I pulled the remote control from the nightstand drawer and turned on the television, an ultra slim 55" high definition 3D Samsung television that was mounted on the wall directly in front of the bed. I changed the channel to the Falcons game and turned the volume down. Next to the nightstand, I placed a small bucket of ice filled with four Heinekens, Taz's favorite beer. I showered and put on the one suit Taz loves to see me in - a tan Zanetti suit with matching vest, tie, and shoes.

I heard the garage door open and Max's engine slow to a hushed silence. The car door slammed shut and the garage door closed shortly after. Taz always came in the house through the front door after checking through the local advertisements, sales coupons, and junk mail. I listened as she walked up the three short steps leading to the front door. I was there just in time to open the door for her and sing the chorus of Gerald Levert's "Mr. Too Damn Good." She smiled and dropped her keys along with everything else she had in her hand on the table as I greeted her with a kiss and an ice cold Heineken.

My plans to make Taz give in to me were suddenly changed. Things went in a completely different direction. Instead of Taz just going with the flow like I wanted her to, she took control. She pushed her way through the doorway and stood directly in front of me. She grinned, but her facial expressions revealed something very unfamiliar. I was seeing a completely different side of her, one that I had been waiting to come out for a while. She took a sip of beer, grabbed me by my tie, and led me to the bedroom.

"You know what I want you to do?" she asked boldly with a deep voice.

"No, but I'm sure you'll tell me," I replied.

"Hmmm," she sighed. "Take off the jacket."

"Make me," I responded as I stared into her eyes with excitement.

"Not today. Just do it," she replied in a stern voice, but I continued to challenge her.

The next thing I knew, Taz grabbed me by the arm, pulled my jacket off, and threw it over the armchair next to the dresser. She loosened my tie and unbuttoned my shirt. I was left there with just my slacks, shoes, and an A-shirt. Taz was on a roll and I liked it. She finally pushed me to the bed with such force that it startled me.

"You put all that shit on, now take it off," Taz commanded. "Start with the shirt."

Taz was definitely in charge. I pulled my shirt out of my pants and quickly pulled it over my head to take it off.

"Keep the sports bra on," she insisted. "I like seeing you just like that."

I felt good. Since Taz seemed to be too busy for me, I spent a lot of time at The G Spot working out and boxing. After weeks of slacking off, I finally had my six pack abs again, chiseled arms, and well-defined back muscles again. All of that may have just paid off for me in a completely different way.

"Lose MD, too," she said. "I'm not feeling that right now."

Taz's request surprised me. I've never been without MD. It was a part of me. It gave me the look I wanted and made me feel like I was in charge of my life even more. It's what all the ladies liked and a few of the gay men I had business with every now and then. Nevertheless, I submitted to Taz's request.

She sat her beer on a coaster on the nightstand and undressed. Her smooth skin and toned muscles aroused me even more as she walked slowly to Treasure Island and pulled out a black 9" Doc. I watched as she quickly washed it in the bathroom, strapped up, and put on a condom. She was ready and so was I.

She took her time with me. She slowly stroked my legs, arms, breasts, and kissed me on the chest and neck. She placed her hand on my clit and gently fingered me. She kept kissing me and rubbing me all over my body. I closed my eyes and lay there on my back waiting for her next move. Then, she went all in. Her tongue moved across my clit like molasses. Every pass was different than the last one.

I was in another world. She kissed my legs again, rubbed my feet, and then slowly pushed my legs apart. She and Doc made their way inside me. Her actions were slow, steady, and methodical. I felt so in tune with her that I just let myself give in to her. I found myself calling her name for the first time in a very long time. Whatever she wanted me to do at that moment, I did it.

It seemed like hours had gone by. I felt the adrenaline run through my body. It felt like somebody turned the heat up. I was sweating like crazy. I vaguely heard the sportscaster giving the play-by-play action on TV. It was third and long with ten seconds left in the game. The only option the Falcons had was a Hail Mary in the end zone. As Taz spread my legs even more and allowed Doc to go full steam ahead, I heard the crowd scream. The sportscaster yelled, "Rowdy Roddy with a one-hand catch!" I was excited as Taz stepped it up one more notch on Doc. I went all in with her. I made it as easy as possible for her to get whatever angle she wanted to get an orgasm.

     We screamed each other's names and exploded together. We lay there for a few seconds. It had been so long since the last time we had sex. It's sad to think about it, but at that point, I knew Nic had nothing on Taz. It was almost like Taz was a whole new person. I couldn't understand it, but it didn't matter. I kept hearing the sportscaster say something, but I couldn't make out the words. It was all good. I just scored the ultimate touchdown.

# Action!

*It seemed there were a million people around us and our table was on center stage. There were no spotlights or movie cameras or someone to say, "cut" and rescue us. At that very moment, I anticipated a huge close-up on my life and nothing shy of a total blackout could save us.*

## Chapter 9

      It was getting late and Preacher still hadn't arrived for Taz's birthday dinner at Michael's. Everyone else was on time, including Taz's faithful Blackjack crew. As Taz and her friends talked, I listened with mild discontent. A feeling of nostalgia came over me.

      As I looked over the staircase leading to the main lobby, I thought about what happened between Taz and me in the lockerroom. It was the first time Taz truly gave in to me and I didn't have to force anything to happen. It seemed she had let go of any insecurities she had at the time and allowed herself to be tamed. Unfortunately, it was also the moment when everything between us shifted and our business became part of a never-ending battle.

"What's up everybody? Where's the birthday boy?" Preacher shouted as she walked toward the back where we were holding a shiny blue gift bag.

"Hey Preacher, why are you so late?" Taz asked. "You missed the first two rounds of Goose."

"I had to take care of something," Preacher replied as she looked in my direction. "I got some news that just couldn't wait."

"Is everything okay?" Taz asked.

"It's all good, Timeka," Preacher quickly responded. "It's nothing you need to worry about."

Preacher continued to look in my direction. I listened as Roz, Redd, Jesse, and Shy talked about the women in their lives. I was surprised. Jesse had a new flame every week and Roz just didn't seem like the type to appreciate any woman, even for a moment. Shy, on the other hand, was content with her girlfriend of four years and even talked about tying the knot in D.C. next year.

"Marriage isn't for me," Taz proclaimed.

"Why not?" Shy asked. "Maybe you haven't found the right woman."

"Well, I'm glad Reece is history," Jesse interrupted. "I didn't like her ass anyway. Everything about her was fake. Everything from her hair down to her stank-attitude had a price tag on it."

"So why don't you have a woman?" Redd asked Taz.

"Fuck a woman! They're just trouble anyway," Roz said and took a sip of beer. "Don't get sucked in, Taz, unless you want your very own ball and chain telling you what to do for the rest of your life."

Taz remained quiet. I could tell she was uneasy. But, I was curious myself as I waited for Taz's response to Redd's question. The thought of marriage never crossed my mind, at least not a second time. I was married once to a beautiful girl named Kim for almost three years. We never had a ceremony at a big church with a big reception, but we considered ourselves soul mates. We exchanged rings in front of our friends at a dinner party and that was it. We shared everything. We were about to close on our first home until the unthinkable happened. Nic.

Nic came into my life unexpectedly. I was in the middle of planning my future and Nic uprooted all that I had done. My life changed. Nic was also the one thing I needed to help me come to terms with what I really wanted and move into a space where I was more comfortable. Kim and I found a way to remain friends, but that was it. We knew there could never be anything else between us again. After a while, we lost touch altogether.

"Yeah, Timeka," Preacher interrupted. "What are you waiting for? Surely, there's somebody."

"Look, I'm just not ready," Taz said.

"Well, there is somebody, right?" Preacher asked.

Everyone was quiet. Taz looked nervous and tried to play it off by changing the subject. They went along with it, but it wasn't long before words turned into silence and silence turned into sharp tension. I tried to keep my composure. I wanted to hear an answer, too, but I didn't want to cause any trouble. It was Taz's birthday and I wanted her to have fun.

"Timeka, why don't you tell us?" Preacher inquired. "Why are you keeping secrets?"

"Let it go, man!" Taz demanded and stared at Preacher.

"Guys," Preacher said.. "Haven't you noticed that wherever Timeka is, her shadow is nearby?"

"What the hell are you talking about, Preacher?" Redd and Shy asked simultaneously.

"Preach!" Taz exclaimed. "Drop it!"

"Timeka and this chocolate suit next to me are a couple. Right after Reece took a hike, and I'm glad she did too, these two became an item of sorts."

Everyone stopped eating and drinking and all eyes were on me and Taz. If ever there was a time I wished I could be somewhere else, this was that moment. Their

113

stares were hard and unyielding. The silence was unbearable. Taz looked at me with fear in her eyes and all I could do was stare back at her. There wasn't much I could say. I didn't know what to say. It seemed there were a million people around us and our table was on center stage. There were no spotlights or movie cameras or someone to say, "cut" and rescue us. At that very moment, I anticipated a huge close-up on my life and nothing shy of a total blackout could save us. Preacher just sat back watching to see how the scene would turn out.

"Well, there goes the fucking neighborhood!" Roz finally said and laughed, breaking the silence and easing some of the tension. "If you like it, pop the top and turn it up, bruh. Pussy is still pussy when all the lights are off and the music's playing. Shit, you just got yourself a little thug pussy. I ain't had none of that! But, I'm good, don't hurt yourself trying to hook me up."

"Shut up, Roz! You're kidding, Taz?" Jesse asked. "What's up?"

"It's true," Taz confessed after what seemed like an eternity. "Silk is my--"

Jesse stopped Taz mid-sentence. "Don't say it. That's crazy, man. You're dating this nigga?"

Taz looked me in the eyes. She seemed confused and hesitant to keep talking.

"What's wrong with you?" I asked Jesse. "You got a problem?"

Jesse stood up quickly and so did I. She stood directly in front of me and looked at me with contempt. Taz tried to calm us both down.

"Yeah! I have a problem. And it can kiss my ass. I'm outta here."

Jesse grabbed her things and left. Preacher just sat there, still drinking wine with a peculiar grin on her face. Redd and Shy were speechless as their eyes opened wide in disbelief. Taz tried to stop Jesse, but it was no use. She watched as Jesse walked down the stairs and carelessly bumped into two trainers as they were leaving the front lobby.

"So, Silk is your woman, man, whatever you want to call her?" Shy asked.

"Yes," Taz assured her.

"Okay, okay," Redd said dryly. "Why didn't you tell us this before?"

"I don't know. I didn't think you'd understand. I guess I was right," Taz replied.

"You're damn right," Redd said. "And I probably never will understand this. You're a stud and Silk's one shape-up from being a real man." She hesitated momentarily, stared at me with a look of confusion, and resumed speaking in a more relaxed voice. "I don't get this, but I'm not the one who has to get it in the ass."

"What about you, Shy?" Taz asked.

"I'm good," Shy replied. "Do what you do, but don't expect me to come to any weddings."

"Wanna know what I think?" Roz interrupted. "I say fuck it, two studs in bucket. Why should I care about what you do? It's not my bucket. I still got your back, man."

"Well, isn't this wonderful?" Preacher said sarcastically.

"Why did you do this?" I asked Preacher. "And today of all days, why?"

"I'm tired of the bullshit, that's why!" Preacher's tone was noticeably different. She spoke with anger and concern in her voice. She paused then looked at each one of us at the table, took another sip of wine, and continued.

"Timeka, if this is the man you want to be with, so be it. The people still sitting here at this table don't give a rat's ass what you do, or who you do, when you get home. You keep running around here playing games and trying to hide shit. You deserve an award for all the acting you've been doing around here lately."

Roz chimed in sarcastically. "You 'bout to make me cry, dude. Have a drink."

For the next two hours or so, we talked about how Taz and I met, the girls, sports, and my boxing career. It was relaxing. It was like a huge burden was lifted off my shoulders and I no longer had to prove myself to

Preacher or fight for acceptance. Taz seemed okay. I figured she was worried and upset about how Jesse felt, but that was an issue for another day. By the end of the night, I felt much closer to Taz and I finally felt like I was a part of the group. But that feeling of euphoria was tragically taken from me when I said good night to Preacher in the parking lot.

"Hey, thanks," I said and stretched out my hand to her.

"I don't want your appreciation. But, I do need your help. I'll call you with the details."

# Table Talk

*"Zodiac had you on a short chain with little room to move. You were her Tina and she was your Ike, relatively speaking of course. Your job was to sing the song and don't ask questions." She paused momentarily, laughed, then resumed. "But, I understand. You gotta do what you gotta do."*

## *Chapter 10*

I waited for Preacher at Starbucks. I sat at a small corner table by the window and watched as cars circled the parking lot. Some people chose to sit outside and enjoy the unusually hot and humid weather. Others seemed content with their favorite grande selection at their side while surfing the web or talking business. A few people indulged in the sweet smells of pumpkin spice, cinnamon, and hazelnut, even though a few minutes in the sun could only help them. After about ten minutes, I saw Preacher park her black and chrome-trimmed Denali next to my Nissan. She was dressed to the nines in a pair of tan slacks, brown alligator shoes and an Italian style polo shirt as she walk hurriedly inside. She placed her order at the counter, counted her change, and finally sat down at my table.

"So, what's going on Preacher? You couldn't tell me what the big deal was on the phone?"

"I'm fine, how are you?" she asked sarcastically.

I sighed. "Hey," I said reluctantly. I really wanted to walk away. I thought this was just another way of her making my life miserable and cause problems between me and Taz. She didn't like me for whatever reason so I learned to keep my distance as much as possible.

"We have a problem," Preacher finally said. "A huge problem."

"How do 'we' have a problem?" I inquired and waited anxiously for a response.

"Listen," Preacher said calmly. "You and I got off on the wrong foot. Perhaps we can be friends."

"Friends?" She caught me by surprise and I

immediately got in defense mode. I knew something was about to go down.

"Yes, friends," she replied. "The way I see it, circumstances have brought us together at such a time as this to be allies, not enemies."

"What are you talking about? I have other things to do," I politely told Preacher in hopes that she'd hurry up and say whatever was on her mind.

"Word has it that Timeka is in deep with some people who just don't like their business in the streets. Word also has it that everything is centered around you."

I remained silent. Suddenly, everything she was saying faded into a distant blur and the only thing I could focus my attention on was Taz and what kind of trouble she managed to find again. I thought about Nic and what happened at the mall. I was certain I'd have to make good on my promise to her. I became silently outraged as I watched Preacher lean back in her seat and calmly open two packs of Splenda. She emptied them one at a time into her cup, put the lid on, and smiled slyly.

"So, what is it like being a prostitute, or is there another word for what you do?"

She calmly blew through the tiny hole in the coffee lid as the steam slowly vanished. From nearby tables, I could feel the curious stares and wandering ears trying to tune in to our conversation. A young college guy who sat at the table next to us suddenly stopped typing feverishly on his laptop and just stared at the screen as if he was really concentrating on his next sentence. A middle-age woman looked at us both strangely as she slowly rocked her baby in a tiny stroller. She tried to look down, but I caught a glimpse of her curious eyes and knew Preacher was about to go all in if I didn't say something.

"You must have me confused with someone else," I lied.

"I don't think so. I did a little research." She leaned in closer and spoke a little quieter. "I know about the hustle you had going on with Zodiac. From all the way back to your days in backwoods Mississippi to now,

123

you've been fucking top-dolla hoes and showing men how to control the pussy they were getting. You must have been good at it. You have that nice ass house, clothes for days, and I haven't seen you do a day's work yet. I still don't know why you're cruisin in that beat up Nissan, but that's a different story. Zodiac had you on a short chain with little room to move. You were her Tina and she was your Ike, relatively speaking of course. Your job was to sing the song and don't ask questions." She paused momentarily, laughed, then resumed. "But, I understand. You gotta do what you gotta do."

I didn't respond to her comments. She went on and on about things in my past. She knew about my boxing and basketball career. She knew about my gang life. She knew almost everything there was to know about me. When I asked her how she found out, she reminded me of our very first conversation. She was determined to discover the real me. It seemed she did just that.

"I don't have beef with you, Silk. It's your life and as long as Timeka is cool with it, I'm cool. You came out of nowhere. But right now, you've gotta call off the mob squad in South Carolina. Timeka stirred up some memories most people there wanted to forget."

"What do you mean?" I asked.

"Silk, you're smart. Do you think Nic just showed up one day to spread some holiday cheer? She was in your house and knew about you and Timeka. It wasn't by accident." She paused and glanced out the window then continued. "It took me a minute to figure it out, but I got it."

My mind was racing. I was upset, but unsure where to focus my anger and frustration. All I could do was keep listening to Preacher and hope she made a point very soon so I could leave and pay a visit to Nic.

"Remember Reece? She hated you. She hated you so much, she would sell her mother's soul to the devil and walk through hell for a chance to see you broken down. She felt you came between her and Timeka and she was determined to get even with you. Because of you, she lost her free ride to a rich, comfortable life with Timeka. Just one good contract would set her up on easy street. Then came you. She set things in motion as far as you having to get back in the game with Zodiac, the videotape in the lockerroom, and Nic paying you a friendly visit at the mall. That bitch even had a key to your house. She knew you'd find out about Zodiac's business in South Carolina. What she didn't count on was Timeka. She wasn't in the plan. The focus was supposed to be on you. And now, because of what Reece started, there are some people who want to prove to Timeka that she should just mind her business. Reece is taking a backseat and pretending like nothing ever happened."

"What are you saying, Preacher?" I asked.

I was in shock and didn't know what to do. I wasn't sure what else to say. Visions of my past life came quickly in my head. The calm, sweet smell of coffee blends suddenly changed into the sweet stench of revenge. My heart was racing. My breathing intensified. The adrenaline was racing through my body like a freight train. I knew I had to do something and I knew exactly what I wanted to do.

"I'm saying if you don't want to see the people you care about floating in the Chattahoochee, you'll help me come up with a plan to end this. I may be a jerk sometimes, but when it comes to certain things, I'm the one S.O.B. you don't want to mess with."

# Promises

*I was young and didn't understand it then, but I saw their deaths as a failure to keep a promise. They drilled in our heads to always keep promises or we'd always be considered liars. Since I was a kid, I always told people that if I said it, I meant it and there was never any confusion.*

## Chapter 11

"What's wrong with you?" Taz asked as we got in my car to head back home from Dave and Buster's.

"Nothing at all," I lied and glanced in the rearview mirror at Alex and Taylor, who were both exhausted after playing video games and eating pizza all evening. They had drifted off to sleep with giant teddy bears still in their hands, but neither of them was a sound sleeper.

"You sure?" Taz asked again. "It seems you're a million miles away."

She knew something was wrong, but I wasn't in the mood to talk, especially in front of the girls. Even when there was something wrong, Taz and I knew not to talk about it in front of them. Alex and Taylor were like sponges and soaked up everything they heard. I always wanted them to know what was going on, but some things just weren't meant for kids to hear, especially little girls. For Alex and Taylor, however, there was purpose in every conversation and they wanted to be included.

One day, they overheard us talking about a trip to Washington. It would have been our first real trip together with Taz. Rather than think of it as a mini-getaway in the nation's capital, Taylor's first thought was that we were getting married. At the time, nothing could have been further from the truth. Even though the mere thought of vows between studs seemed like an impossible mission, especially for me and Taz, it wasn't the worse thing in the world that could happen. It just wasn't happening right now.

"Let it go, Taz. I told you I was fine."

She looked at me with a look of concern. I couldn't tell her about my meeting with Preacher even though I wanted to. I wondered if she really knew about Reece and what she was up to. Rather than continue the silence and have her think something was wrong, I casually started talking about plans for the summer and silently wished I could have a smoke.

As we pulled into Twin Oaks, flashing red and blue lights and a crowd of people standing near our front lawns caught our attention. Police officers tried desperately to keep neighbors on the sidewalk and out of harms way while firefighters tried to control the flames. As we got closer to my driveway, I kept looking around trying to find out what was causing so much panic. Reality finally hit me and I was faced with certain tragedy.

I parked the car on the side of the street and watched in disbelief as Mrs. Carter's house was reduced to nothing more than a memory amid smoldering wood.

"Damn!" Taz shouted as she instructed the girls to go home and lock the doors.

I ran over thinking I could save her. I thought that what I was witnessing was just a horrible dream. Taz tried to hold me back, but I forced my way out of her grasp and raced toward Mrs. Carter's house. Just as I sped past the ash-stained daisies that lined the mailbox, someone grabbed me.

"There's nothing you can do!" I heard a deep, unfamiliar voice say as I kept trying to break free. "It was too late to save her. I'm sorry."

I looked at the man standing in front of me. His face was dirty. He took off his hat, placed it under his arm, and apologized again. Then, he walked away as if nothing ever happened. I fell to my knees and cried. For the first time since my sister died, I felt alone again. I sat there surrounded by weeping neighbors, sirens, and the crisp echoes of flashing flames, but all I heard was silence. Taz knelt down beside me and tried to comfort me. She couldn't possibly understand what I was feeling.

I thought about the first time I met Mrs. Carter. The big Sunday dinners we enjoyed at her house and the conversations we had on the front porch sipping sweet iced tea meant something to me. The first time I tasted peach preserves on a hot, buttery biscuit reminded me of being home. I felt like my Mama and Pops never left. To me, Mrs. Carter was their way of keeping their promise to always be there for us. I was young and didn't understand it then, but I saw their deaths as a failure to keep that promise. They drilled in our heads to always keep promises or we'd be considered liars. Since I was a kid, I always told people that if I said it, I meant it.

"Leave me alone!" I yelled at Taz and looked up one more time at what was left of Mrs. Carter's house.

I was angry. This couldn't have been some random accident. After talking with Preacher, I was almost certain that what happened here tonight was planned and designed to get my attention. It worked.

133

"I need a minute," I told Taz sharply as she stood and watched the firefighters unhook their hoses and get back on their firetrucks. She nodded her head and walked away.

As the last firetruck drove out of Twin Oaks, I noticed a police car parked on the side of the street. Its lights were still flashing. I assumed the officer had to know what was going on and maybe had a suspect in mind. I walked toward what used to be Mrs. Carter's screened in porch hoping to get some answers from the police. I stopped in my tracks and felt my heart sink fast. Out of the ashes and smoke, I saw the police officer escorting a familiar face. It was Zodiac.

"What are you doing here?" I yelled as I rushed over to where Zodiac was standing. "Did you do this?"

The officer stopped me before I could say anything else. "Ms. Carter, do you know this person?" the officer asked Zodiac.

"Carter?" I said under my breath.

134

"She probably didn't tell you, Silk," Zodiac said as she fought back tears. "I'm her granddaughter."

# Suited Up

*I tried to do the right thing, but the gun went off by mistake. I tried to save her, but it was too late. She died in my arms on a Tuesday night. Sometimes I wonder if everything that happened in my life since that night was my fault and I was being punished by an angry God who really wanted me to pay for everything I did wrong.*

## Chapter 12

   Preacher and I agreed to meet in the parking lot
at the Sheraton Hotel where Taz was being recognized by
the Lesbian Lawyers Association. She was being awarded
the Gold Gavel Award for helping openly gay and lesbian
high school athletes get into college. She looked forward
to it all month. She told everybody who'd listen about her
big night. She bought a new suit from Brooks Brothers,
diamond cufflinks, and new snake skin shoes. She even
called Fred, her colleague who has a mobile auto detail
business, to give Max the royal treatment. Instead of

waiting on her all day, we agreed to meet in the hotel lobby at 6:30.

I was happy for Taz, but my mind was in another place. It was a sad time for me. It had been a week since the fire and we still didn't know who was behind it. As evil as Zodiac was, I couldn't make myself believe she had anything to do with it. Then it hit me. It must have been Reece. Based on what Preacher said, she was the only likely suspect.

"Will Uncle T get a trophy?" Taylor asked.

"Maybe," I replied.

As we drove along, Alex and Taylor kept asking questions about Taz and the kind of things that might happen tonight at the awards dinner. As always, they were curious and wanted to know everything. Alex and Taylor meant the world to me. I saw more and more of my sister in them every day. They've grown up so much over the years, even with everything that's been going on. I knew Debbie would be proud of the young women they've become.

For a long time, I blamed myself for Debbie's death. If it wasn't for me trying to live a street life, a life that really wasn't for me anyway, she never would've died. I tried to do the right thing, but the gun went off by mistake. I tried to save her, but it was too late. She died in my arms on a Tuesday night. Sometimes I wonder if everything that happened in my life since that night was my fault and I was being punished by an angry God who really wanted me to pay for everything I did wrong.

I was almost at the hotel when I heard a loud explosion and my rims screeching across the pavement. I had a flat tire just across the street near the basketball court where Taz and I first shot hoops together. Except for a few empty water bottles strewn carelessly across the baseline, the court was empty. The streetlights were turned off, leaving only the glow of dim sunlight to strike against the red and black asphalt. I asked the girls if they were alright, stepped outside, and opened the trunk to get the spare tire. I was mad that I was dressed in one of my favorite Dior suits and had to change a dirty tire. I wanted to light a Black and Mild, but I didn't. Instead, I placed my jacket on the back of the front seat and got to work.

It was killing me not knowing what was going on. Preacher had all the answers. I had to rely on her for all of them. I was still caught up with the image of Zodiac leaving Mrs. Carter's house. I was sickened by the thought that Reece would have the balls to murder anybody. I was angry, on the edge, and needed closure.

"That's what I like about you, man," I heard Preacher say as she appeared out of nowhere and startled me. "You're a man's man. Who needs triple A when they've got you?"

"What the hell are you doing here?" I asked as Preacher walked over in a black suit and shirt, red tie and pocket square, and a red trimmed hat.

"I noticed you and this piece of metal you call a car on my way to the hotel and thought you might need

140

some help."

"Whatever," I replied. "As long as you're here, you can tell me what's going on. You didn't really tell me much on the phone."

"Patience, Denzel. Patience," she replied sarcastically.

Patience was the one thing I ran out of. It was no longer a part of me. All that was left was anxiety, frustration, and anger.

"What the hell is going on, Preacher?" I threw the crowbar on the ground. I leaned the spare tire against the car, but it slowly wobbled its way to the ground between us. Preacher took a step back and gave me a few more details.

The plan was to show up prepared for anything, even if it meant bringing a gun. That wasn't my style. I knew how to handle myself and I knew the streets enough to know that nothing big would go down in a room of people. It was safe.

"I'm sorry about the fire. Timeka told me how close you guys were." Preacher stopped momentarily. "You know, you really shouldn't have brought the girls here tonight." She peeked through the back driver-side window, smiled, and waved at the girls. "This could get ugly."

"What do you mean?"

"I don't know all the details, but I got a feeling this dinner is about more than just an award. It's quite possible that whoever Timeka pissed off will be here tonight. I hope you're ready."

She seemed ready for a fight. She moved from making sarcastic attacks against me to being more serious. She looked at me with great concern in her eyes and then walked away. My first instinct was to take Alex and Taylor back home because Preacher made me feel uneasy about them being at the dinner. At the same time, I've never been the type to run away from a challenge. I changed the tire, brushed the dirt off my hands, and was on my way.

# Rookies

*"One of my favorite movies is Training Day. You know the one where Denzel's partner is a rookie cop and he tries to show him the ropes by taking him out in the field for a few hours? My favorite scene is when Denzel shot the old man at his house, took his money, and then told his partner, 'gimme the bitch.'"*

## Chapter 13

"Well, well, well," I heard a voice say from the shadows of a dark corner as we walked into a large empty ballroom. "Tonight's special guest has arrived."

Taz and I looked at each other in disbelief. Alex and Taylor asked if we were in the right place. The room was dimly lit and quiet. There were no tables and no movement. I looked at my watch. It was almost 7:00.

"Who's that?" Taz asked hesitantly.

"Baby, surely you remember me."

It was Reece. She slowly stepped out of the shadows wearing a sexy red strapless dress and red heels.

She walked with an attitude that said she ruled the universe and we were just pawns on a chessboard. She was still beautiful, but with more style, class, and elegance. Suddenly the lights got a little brighter and we were standing face-to-face with the devil.

"What the hell are you doing here?" Taz questioned. "What is this?"

"Tonight is all about you, baby," Reece said. "We're here to recognize you for all of your wonderful accomplishments this year."

It took everything in me not to just go off. In my mind, Reece was my opponent in the ring. She was the one keeping me from that championship title I worked so hard for. She was the one thing interfering with my happiness. She was the one thing that stood between me and Taz. As much as I wanted to loosen up my tie and go head-to-head with her, I didn't. I just sat back and watched and held the girls closer to me.

"Would you like some champagne?" Reece asked

Taz and then looked at me briefly. She never spoke.

"No, I don't," Taz replied.

"You could at least have some champagne, baby," Reece said and motioned for a tray. "It took a lot of hard work to make this happen for you tonight. A few phone calls, some cozy dinners, and a whole lot of negotiation went into this just to get you here tonight. Surely you don't want all this planning to go to waste."

"You know what," Taz said and turned to walk away. "I'm not doing this tonight. Let's go, guys."

I kept my eyes on Reece for a few more moments then turned to walk away. Reece had people standing at the door to keep us from leaving. I couldn't believe who I saw standing before me. It was Nic and her crew, Preacher, and a couple people I didn't know. They were all dressed in black suits, red ties, and black dress shoes. Suddenly the old me came out and I couldn't contain myself anymore. I was ready to fight.

"What the fuck is this?" I screamed at Reece. "My

kids are here."

I quickly stepped toward Reece, but was stopped by some braided up stud in a black overcoat who showed me the gun she had in her inside coat pocket. It didn't scare me. It wouldn't have been the first time somebody pulled a gun on me.

"I missed you, Silk," Reece said. "It's too bad we couldn't be friends."

"Fuck you," I replied.

Reece smiled and resumed whatever game she was trying to play. "Yes, you did that, Silk. And rather nicely as I recall. Speaking of friends, you remember Nic, don't you?"

"What is she talking about?" Taz asked me. "Who's Nic?"

Nic walked in, stood next to Reece, and grinned. Reece was in the zone now. She was probably thinking she had us right where she wanted us. In a way, she did. "Silk, don't tell me you've been keeping this fine ass a secret from Taz. I thought you two were beyond that by now. Come on, what are you hiding?"

"What is she talking about?" Taz asked again as she stared at Nic and Reece. "What's going on here?"

"Baby," Reece said in a low voice. "Nic is Silk's ex. They were in love once upon a time, much like you and I were. They've spent some time together as of late, but I'm sure Silk told you about that."

Taz's face lost all expression. She looked at me with disdain. "I trusted you," she finally said as she shoved me. "Really? After everything that's happened between us! That's fucked up!"

"You don't understand. She's lying," I said.

Reece interrupted. "I thought we had a good thing going, baby. I gave my all to you. I loved you. I made you. You wouldn't have half the shit you have now if it wasn't for me. I brought AJ and other top names to you on a silver platter, but you blew it. Big time people like that don't like being caught up in big time drama. That

148

day I saw you in the grocery store with these two precious little girls, I gave you one more chance at happiness and you blew that, too. Frankly, I'm fed up."

The girls were getting scared. I tried to calm them down a little and assure them that everything would be fine. They stood behind me and grabbed my leg tightly.

Nic took a few steps toward me. "Damn, why did you put me in this position?" she asked. "I told you that if you kept your boy on a short leash, there'd be no problem. Now, I got a problem."

"Nic, I told you that if you come near them, I'd kill you myself." My tone was firm and I looked directly in her eyes as I spoke.

Nic laughed and looked at Taz. "Why did you have to go snooping around? We were just minding our own business and having a good time until you came along. I hope you got what you came for."

The girls became more agitated and scared. I wanted them to be anywhere but here at this very moment. I looked at Preacher, but I wasn't sure what side she was on. For the first time in a long time, I was scared, nervous, and looking for a way out.

All of a sudden, Nic gave me a familiar look. It was a look we shared a few times before when we were both hustlin'. It was a look that said "trust me," but I was not in the frame of mind to trust anyone in the room with me, especially Nic. I couldn't even trust myself at that very moment.

The long stare between Nic and I was cut short by a slamming door. I heard another familiar voice. I looked back at the doors where Preacher was standing and saw Zodiac enter the room. I didn't know how to react to her or what to say. I didn't tell anyone I saw her at the fire. All I knew was this whole situation was getting worse by the minute.

"Taz, it's so good to see you," Zodiac said as she walked gracefully into the room, stood by Reece, and kissed her on the cheek. "I apologize for my tardiness. I had some unfinished business to take care of. If you want something done right, sometimes you have to do it yourself. You know how that goes."

"Honey," Reece said to Zodiac. "We're just about done here."

"I'm sorry we had to meet like this, Taz," Zodiac said as she opened her purse and pulled out a tube of lip stick and a mirror. "The last time we spoke, Counselor, I told you I'm not the one to be played with."

"I thought guys liked to be played with," Taz responded. Zodiac looked over the top of her mirror, smiled, and continued with her touch-up."

"You know what, this isn't looking good for you right now," I told Taz. "You should just shut the fuck up."

Zodiac walked over to Taz. They stared at each other for what seemed like hours, but they never spoke a word. Then, Zodiac's attention turned to me. Still, she never said a word. All I heard was Reece chuckling in the background next to Nic.

"You know what, boys?" Zodiac said as she stood in front of us wearing a tight black skirt, matching blazer, and boots. "One of my favorite movies is *Training Day.* You know the one where Denzel's partner is a rookie cop and he tries to show him the ropes by taking him out in the field for a few hours? My favorite scene is when Denzel shot the old man at his house, took his money, and then told his partner, 'gimme the bitch' and they gave him this big ass shotgun."

"What do you want, Zodiac?" I asked.

"Gimme the bitch," Zodiac said and continued to smile at us. Nic walked over with a Smith and Wesson 40mm handgun with a pink handle and gave it to Zodiac.

"Wait, I don't know what kind of bullshit you've got going on right now, but this is not a movie. Let my kids go and then we can settle this grown folks style."

Before I could finish speaking, Preacher walked up and grabbed the girls by the hand. She looked at me just as strangely as Nic did and then led the girls outside to the lobby area.

We all stood there in the middle of the ballroom not sure what was happening. Zodiac loaded the clip, smiled at us one more time, and then quickly pointed the gun at Reece.

"Baby girl," she said as Reece 's chuckles turned into silence. "You will never be as good at this game as I am. You are a rookie. I don't care what these dykes did to you. You tried to play me. You thought that you could use me to get even with Taz because she dumped you. Bitch, I would've dumped your trifling ass, too. I know everything."

I didn't know what was happening. Everything just turned into a big blur as I heard guns clicking all around the room, each one pointed at somebody. I looked around again to make sure the girls were nowhere in sight. I heard a shot fire and then the room went black.

Stay Tuned...

# Acknowledgments

I would like to first thank God for giving me a clear mind and opening up opportunities for me to complete this book. Every day was a struggle, but you never left my side. I've often questioned "why me?" but you helped me redefine my life and ask "why not me?" Thank you!

LaShundria, my beautiful, loving wife, you are the wind that keeps me sailing. I love you with all my heart. Through all the trials and challenges we've had over the past couple years, I've found that no one could ever replace what we have together. You are my friend, my confidante, and my everything! You are also my biggest supporter and cheerleader. If I had nothing else in the world but you, I'd still be the richest and happiest person in the world.

Q, stay focused! The world is yours if you'd just take a moment to reach out and grab it.

Mocha, since this entire series began, our friendship has grown. I appreciate you very much. Thanks for letting me bounce ideas off of you. Most importantly, thanks for helping keep me on track and helping me realize everything has a purpose.

I would like to extend a very special thanks to Kai "The Stud Slayer" Brown from Washington, D.C. Thanks for shedding light on a subject most of us in the Black GLBT community, including myself, never knew about until now. I have gained a much deeper appreciation for the uniqueness of S4S relationships. The things people choose to ignore or belittle are oftentimes the most valuable sources of knowledge, strength, and empowerment. I hope that by the time people have read the entire Strapped series, they, too, will step outside the box as you and many others have and live in truth.

To Tangela and Santoinette Baker, I would like to extend a special thanks to you for all you have done. San, at times, my faith was tested and you stepped in at the right moment to remind me that God is bigger than my situation. That one statement was enough to get me through some difficult times. Tangie, you are more than just my sister. You are a constant reminder of what friendship, loyalty, and dedication are supposed to look like. God gave you the gift to gab and be funny, but He also gave you the ability to encourage, motivate, and inspire others. I love you guys and I appreciate you so much. San, I can't go to Pluto with you. They don't have Cokes and chocolate chip cookies out there. That's not a happy place for me!

Thanks to all of my other brothers and sisters for all of your support and prayers. Sly, Ebony, CeeJay, Kandace, Yolanda, BG, DJ, Ebonee, Selena, Jay, and the whole gang – you guys are awesome!

To Alex, Epitamy, Malik, Jazzy, Tasha, E., and the entire Santiago Family, you guys ROCK! Many of the ATL families were established to provide a place of refuge and camaraderie for people who may have strained relationships with their own biological families. Each one of you gives new meaning to the word "family." You

157

reached out to me and my family, provided love and support, and helped make each day a whole lot better.

Thanks BG Promotions, Inc. No matter what was going on, you made sure everyone knew! Thanks for promoting me locally and nationally. I look forward to working with you again.

To everyone whose name I didn't mention, you guys are great, too. I appreciate your time and efforts. Friends are a dime a dozen, but true friends are priceless!

To all of the readers and supporters of the Strapped trilogy, THANK YOU! It's my hope that you have learned something new about yourself and others. Please know that your purchase is not just helping someone deal with their own issues, insecurities, or challenges involved with S4S relationships and societal norms. Your purchase is also helping women, and men, from all backgrounds fight breast cancer.

As more women and men are diagnosed with this disease, science, technology, and education have helped increase survival rates. Remember, cancer doesn't discriminate against age, gender, race, or economic class. It can strike people on Wall Street, Main Street, and your street. Find out more about your family's medical history. Encourage the people you know and love to do a monthly breast self-exam. If you don't know how to do it, talk with your doctor or other healthcare professional. You're the expert when it comes to your own body so speak up when you notice changes. Five minutes could save your life. Together, we can find a cure for breast cancer.

# About the Author

Sharon D. Smith is the author of two previously published novels, Love and Liberation (2007) and Strapped (2009). She is the Founder and Chief Editor of Seven Stages Publishing House, LLC. Sharon has plans to write her first business book, *Morning Coffee,* which is scheduled for release in late 2012. The book will be about people who work in the human services industry. It will focus primarily on motivation, leadership, and personal development.

Sharon is a graduate of McNair Sr. High School, Georgia State University, and the University of Phoenix. She is currently a Ph.D. candidate at the University of Phoenix. In her free time, Sharon enjoys playing golf, chess, listening to country music, and watching action movies and crime dramas.

To learn more about Sharon, book events, appearances, or to network, follow her at Facebook.com/Strapped, Facebook.com/Author Sharon D. Smith, or Twitter.com/Strapped2009. You may also send an email to 7stagespublishing@gmail.com.